MW00389153

Demarginalizing Design

Elevating Equity for Real-World Problem Solving

DEE LANIER

Copyright © 2022 Lanier Learning.

Version 1.8.5

All rights reserved. This book or any portion thereof may not be reproduced or used in any manner whatsoever without the express written permission of the publisher except for the use of brief quotations in a book review.

To Karis, Landis, Ellis, and Silas. Y'all have my heart.
Thank you for being the most compassionate and big-hearted
children a dad could have. Mom and I love you forever.

Table of Contents

FORWARD

Flowers From a Friend

"Tomorrow, our seeds will grow.
All we need is dedication."
– Lauryn Hill

I feel incredibly grateful whenever I get a chance to learn from Dee Lanier. Whether it is face-to-face in a full auditorium or in a small virtual group, Dee has a way to make everyone in the room not only feel included, but also make them feel they belong. Once he makes sure we - learners from various positionalities, backgrounds, and experiences - know we fit, he challenges us to solve the most important problems we can possibly imagine. In this, he is caring for our intellect, caring for our hearts, and caring for our dreams of more justice-oriented school communities. Now, with *Demarginalizing Design*, you not only have the opportunity to learn from Dee, you also have the opportunity to create meaningful partnerships with the communities you serve to design learning spaces where we all thrive.

Dr. Val Brown

INTRODUCTION

My Perspective in Prose

"If there's a book you really want to read, but it hasn't been written yet, then you must write it."
– Toni Morrison

Why I wrote this... 'cause schools kinda suck. Hear me out. Schools kinda suck for those that are stuck in the margins- those who were never a part of the original plan for success. Let that sink in. Schools were not designed to foster the success of all students. More food for thought, schools are not failing. Schools are succeeding exactly as they were designed, which means their design is the fundamental problem. Schools were not designed to help Black and Brown kids succeed. They were designed to help white students succeed, achieve, and maintain upward mobility. If you wish to debate that statement, just check the stats. With over 80% of the teacher workforce being white, and in many settings, the Black and Brown population is the inverse.[1] The problem is exacerbated by the cultural disconnection between students and teachers. The solution, in a word, is more equitable practices. If you are unaware or in denial of the problem, you lack empathy for the students and families affected by the problem. Hence this book.

Before you get all big mad and in a huff, know that I do not mean to indict all schools everywhere. Not every classroom, not every teacher, not every district, but as a whole, schools across the United States (and many beyond its border) are rife with inequities from top to bottom. From what I have experienced and what I have been shown, and from what I hear from everywhere- schools suck. And they have for a very long time. Forgive the crude language, but it's what I would say if I were given a microphone while sitting on a panel with professionals way more credentialed than me. I would say it plain, 'cause that's how students share it with me when given full license to speak freely. Go ahead and ask a middle school student what they think about school. Some may call it "ok," others may say, "pretty good," but if we read between the lines and cut across the bull, knowing that they are filtering their language simply out of respect, we would hear, "it sucks." Ask an honest student who doesn't care if they offend you, one who doesn't have anything to lose because they feel they are already lost. They just may say that school straight-up sucks. And you should listen to them. That student is giving you gold. They are telling you the truth, and if you choose not to be offended and simply ask more questions, that student may have more gold to share at the end of the colorful rainbow of language they use.

The reality is the deeper we understand the problem, the better we can prepare to solve it. If we're not ready to hear that there are problems, we're not ready to be problem-solvers, but rather, people who perpetuate the problem. Let's choose to be problem-solvers. Let me start things off by admitting that I may not be respected as a world-renowned researcher on the topic of school improvement. So, what qualifies me to speak on said topic? Besides my degrees in Sociology- yes, that's plural, but pluralistically speaking- experience is my education. My education is my experience. I'm not even referencing the number of years that I have worked in or with schools that serve the underserved or the affluent ones that attempted to diversify their staff. While growing up in various areas in Southern California to eventually traveling the world as a military dependent, I experienced some of the best and worst education our school systems have to offer. I was often transient between schools and households, moving back and forth between my mom in San Diego and grandparents in South Central Los Angeles. Later, my mother joined the military, which took me on a journey through several different schools before I finally finished high school in Wiesbaden, Germany. I did the math and realized that I attended 13 different schools during my K-12 experience. 13! Like I said, I got to see some of the best and worst of education.

In my early years, I would describe my educational experience as mostly boring at best and, in some cases, trauma-inducing. However, sports and a healthy social life kept me sane. Eventually, school became more manageable as I figured out the formula for success for a young Black man: show up, be quiet, do your homework, cram for tests, rinse and repeat. I mastered all those elements, except the staying quiet part. I also realized that if I did all the other things, I could talk all I wanted. Truth be told, only a select few teachers truly inspired me to want to learn and grow; the rest attempted to coerce me with grades as a means of leveraging my future. Even in college up until grad school, school and learning were a means to what I wanted to do next, not a love in and of itself. I did not know what I wanted to be "when I grew up." I just knew that I wanted to solve the problems of violence and substance abuse in my community. I wanted homelessness to be erased and racism to take a nosedive off a cliff wearing no seat belt. Yeah, I hate racism that much. All I knew was that education was supposed to give me the tools to make a difference in the world, but I didn't see how.

When I eventually became a teacher in an alternative high school, I made it my mission to connect to my students in order to help them learn whatever the content. The problem was I found that I was replicating the poor pedagogical practices of my past without even realizing it. I followed the model set before me in my educational experience: I stood at the front of the room with students all in rows looking at me. I fought to keep their attention while teaching from outdated textbooks and constantly threatening to call home or send them to the office. I was the problem, and I didn't even know it.

To the first-year teacher, veteran teacher, school counselor, dean, and principal, I wrote this for you. I wrote this so you could reach students like me. Even after I unlocked the cheat code for success in school, I was plagued by the constant trope, "has potential" written in the comment section of every report card, said at every parent conference, even whispered to me by a teacher after a speech given to my classmates my senior year. It was almost as if my teachers knew that I was not interested in "winning" the game called school they wanted me to play. I could be a 4.0 student. I could do whatever I wanted to do, go to whatever school I wanted to go to, and become whatever profession I pursued if I only cared enough to work harder. My problem is that I did not care. I did not care about Shakespeare, though I cared about love, betrayal, and tragedy. I did not care about the Pythagorean Theorem, but I was striving for balance and proportion in my life. I did not care about conjugations, dangling modifiers, or tense structure, though I was deeply curious about understanding power structures. I did not really care about historical timelines of people who won wars and earned medals for enslaving people who looked like me or freeing people who looked like me from people who looked like them. I was looking for relevance to deeper questions, where the answers could not be found in the back of the book.

Why should I care? I could get by on charm and just enough effort to receive honor and accolades and achieve in academia and athletics. I was shown what success looked like, and the medicine to my mediocrity was simply to try a little harder, but in my eyes, popularity was the only thing worth taking risks for. Maybe because the satisfaction was more immediate, tangible currency, to be liked and loved. I did not know what I wanted to be when I grew up because no one showed me a problem and said that I could be a part of the solution. By 18, I had already achieved more than what society expected of me. I did not fall victim to gang violence, the enticements of slanging dope, or the escapism of getting drunk or high. To the outside world, just surviving was a significant accomplishment given the assumption that I was involved in a gang because of my baggy clothes, unaware that I was the student body president, captain of the football team, and managing editor of the school newspaper. I was potential personified. This is a true story. During my senior year of high school, my mother attended a PTA meeting in which the Military Police gave a presentation on the growing gang culture on base. To her shock, they displayed a picture of me wearing blue baggy sweatpants and a white t-shirt as an example of gang clothing. Our school colors were blue, gold, and white, and I was not a gang member!

It wouldn't be until I attended college that I learned the term "racial profiling", though I experienced it on a daily basis. It would also take a few more years of life experience and educational enlightenment to unlock my empathy for my community and not just myself. I did not know what I wanted to be when I grew up because I did not know what problems were worth solving, so, therefore, what depth of research was required, what anguish would have to be embraced, what collaboration would have to take place- in order to solve it. School was a constant dichotomy- social interaction, laughter, and creativity were mostly reserved for lunchtime, after school, playing sports, and dancing at social functions. The classroom was reserved. Reserved for certain behaviors, such as entering quietly, sitting at a desk, copying what was written on the board, listening to lectures, taking notes, reading aloud, submitting homework, taking quizzes and tests, and scratching the words "I'm bored" onto the desk

To quote former Education Evangelist at Google, Jaime Casap, "Stop asking kids what they want to be when they grow up. Instead, ask them what problems they want to solve, and what they need to solve them." I learned over time that a big problem I wanted to solve was the monotony and lack of relevance of school. I wanted to stop labeling students like me as "having potential" and start helping teachers see their potential instead. If you are a teacher, you have the potential to unlock the passions of pupils like me. If you are an administrator, I believe your first duty is to care for your staff. In my teaching career, I was often subjugated to abusive comments and actions by my leadership before being sent back into spaces with vulnerable children having to experience the presence of a grown man who was treated as a less than. The cycle of trauma continues, and the curse seems generational as adults abuse adults, and then adults abuse children, and those children become adults who have children. If you are in pain, pause, seek the others that are hurting in the margins of your community and find refuge there. Listen to their pain, share your own, and be a human alongside other humans. Hurt sees no hierarchies. Please keep reading if you haven't been too offended by my straight talk thus far. We have a whole lot of problems to solve!

Who Is This For?

If you are wondering if this book is for you, my simple response is, "if not you, then who?" Who needs to read this book and process its content? Who can you read it with to dialogue about the contents, argue with, laugh with, have a heart to heart with? If you are an educator of any stripe, then this book was written with you in mind. You may be a classroom teacher, a building administrator, an instructional coach, or an after-school coordinator. If you are responsible for students' education, safety, and well-being on any level, this book was written with you in mind. You have a perspective, and you operate in a context that will allow you to apply the principles you find in these pages to create a more equitable and enjoyable experience for students and families that often reside in the margins of our educational communities.

Why Are the Margins So Large?

You will note early that this is not a practical how-to guide. This is not a professional development strategy book. This book focuses on the central element of design thinking: thinking. You may have picked up this book because the cover art caused you to pause and look at the many elements and layers of complexity beneath the surface. That's fantastic; keep looking. If you have the paperback version of this book, you may have also noticed that the margins in this book are large and that it is intended to give you the space to reflect and react and write out your questions and share your experience in those spaces that are typically too small to write anything meaningful. I hope you use these margins to draw, plan, express your joy, give room for your pain, and even write out the commitments you will make in light of your journey in this book. I hope you pick this book up often and your future self has a dialogue with your past thinking, and you share how your thinking has changed, how much you still disagree with me, or who you have discussed certain topics with that have deepened your understanding and caused you to listen more closely. Dear educator, use these margins as you wish. There is room for you in and outside of the margins.

How Should You Read This Book?

As many authors often state, I hope you read this book with an open mind. If you are of the mindset that design thinking requires whiteboards, markers, and post-it notes, I would push back and ask the question, "who told you that?" What materials, frameworks, and activities have colonized your creativity so that you understand only one right way to "do" design thinking? I hope that if you initially picked up this book expecting a how-to guide, you are not disappointed, but instead, you are surprised and intrigued enough to keep reading. I do not claim to be on the same level as Dr. Beverly Daniel Tatum, but if you have read her book, *Why Are All the Black Kids Sitting Together in the Cafeteria?* you may have finished it without being able to provide a clear answer to the titular question. The reason why students self-segregate is layered with complexities that require you to learn a lot more and sit with the discomfort of still not fully knowing the answer. More questions need to be asked, and more research needs to be conducted to solve the problems plaguing our educational communities. So that said, I hope that you read this book with not only an open mind, but an open heart. I hope you see the children and their families often underrepresented, given front and center attention. Instead of school conferences before or after school, this is more like the teacher or principal pulling up to the hood to make a house visit and pulling up a chair if welcomed in and learning and listening more than talking.

Practically speaking, I would like to invite all readers to make the following commitments as you read this book. If you are familiar with the "4Cs in Education," I propose the following Commitments in Problem-Solving:

- **Critically think** about your own opinions compared to research and the experiences of others.
- **Collaborate** by seeking to understand and incorporate the voices and talents of others.
- **Communicate** by listening intently and sharing with awareness of verbal and nonverbal language.
- **Creatively** share your ideas in bold, non-traditional ways.

You may be wondering how to commit to that last point while reading a book, so I want to reiterate that I hope you fill the margins here with your own expressions of thought. I hope you add your curious questions, the results of your own research, your own artwork, your own collections! Maybe you agree with some of what I have to say. Maybe you don't. Either way, I hope this work encourages you to be a more responsive listener and learner rather than a reactive one. I hope that you take the time to notice who you are, what power you possess, and what responsibility you have to demarginalize design (even if you are not yet totally clear on that means). My goal isn't to make you feel better. My goal is to make you *feel*, better. Read it again.

Part I

An invitation - Share your thoughts using #DemarginalizingDesign and tag @deelanier on Twitter.

CHAPTER 1

Design Thinking, A Better Way

Chuck Berry made it, but the credit went to Elvis
– Lecrae

How do you Normally Solve Problems?

It's the beginning of the school year, and the staff is attempting to solve a school-wide issue many agree is a problem. So how do you aim to solve it? Throughout my years working in various schools and consulting with numerous districts, I have observed some of the most frequently used problem-solving approaches. Before I list some of those approaches, take a moment to write down or consider how problems are typically addressed in your school setting.

Option one, *Top-Down Decision-Making* is where the problem and solution are proposed altogether. In this approach, an individual or small party huddles, determines the problem and the solution, then delivers it to the majority group responsible for executing the plan. It comes out of the mouth of someone in leadership like this: "Last year we noticed the following problem... so, what we believe will fix this problem is the following solution... any questions?" All the staff that were not a part of the decision-making process begin to roll their eyes

15

because they know that the decision has already been made and that their opinions don't really matter.

Fig 1.1 Top-Down Decision-Making

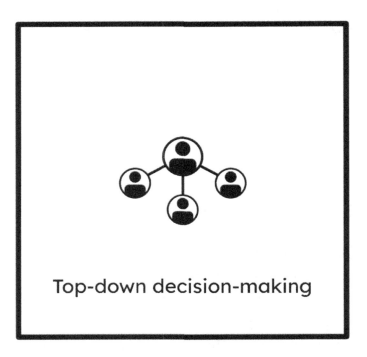

Top-down decision-making

Unfortunately, there is a gap between the people that huddled in isolation to come up with a solution and the staff members responsible for executing the said solution. Some faculty members worry that if they challenge the decision, they are challenging the decision-makers, often their bosses. Every now and then, there is a soon-to-be-retired veteran teacher in the room (with little Fs to give) who challenges the decision loudly, but typically with the resigned statement, "But you've already made your decision, I just don't think it will work!" The admin has anticipated this complaint. They prepared with the naysayer in mind. They respond with, "We hear you. Thank you for that comment. Let's just give it a try." It's a patronizing acknowledgement of the negative viewpoint, without any intention of altering the course of action based on that single complaint. Everyone else will be told in a much more direct manner to comply. It will be sugar-coated with language such as, "we need everyone to be team players" or, "We're asking for everyone to be flexible and adaptable on this one." All the while, many of the staff are thinking, "Who is this *we* you keep speaking of?"

Without community engagement, there is no buy-in. The go-getters (or those without tenure) will do what they can to adhere to the directive in an effort to earn the approval of leadership, while other teachers will only do the bare minimum and wait for the administration to come up with a new solution in the future. The most senior teachers will be the outliers that object altogether, and admin will turn a blind eye to them. Come on now, where's the lie? If you have been fortunate enough to avoid such counterproductive dynamics, you can still reflect on how the dynamics of your community work for you and consider whether that is true for all community members. Though the staff dislikes this top-down approach, it is probably similar to the decision-making process that many teachers use in the classroom with their students. "Here are the class rules," "This is the new procedure," "This is how we will do things moving forward," followed with, "Any questions?" Unfortunately, the top-down approach works in the classroom because the power structures are set up so that compliance is key, and resistance has clear consequences. But where is the buy-in? Even worse, we're producing more of the same. The future leaders are the go-getters that never had any problem conforming or complying with top-down decision making, and everyone else is, well, everyone else.

Unfortunately, a common alternative, what I call the *Faux Democratic Approach*, does not yield much better results. Whether in the staff room or the classroom, this looks to rectify the top-down approach by allowing everyone to respond, but the fact is, not everyone has an equal voice. It usually looks like a facilitator standing at the front of the room and asking everyone to share their thoughts aloud. The leader calls on people in the room to share their ideas, and attendees raise their hands and wait to be recognized before speaking. The leader tries to record all of the shared thoughts, either frantically scribbling to keep up or writing with perfect penmanship to capture every word. Raise your hand if you've witnessed this.

Fig 1.2 Faux Democratic Approach

Faux Democratic Approach

If you have ever sat in a "decision-making" meeting such as this, you know how the dynamics work. Certain people's voices dominate the room with their flurry of ideas; the naysayers raise their hands and offer counter-problems and rationale as to why none of the solutions will actually work, and the rest of the room just idly waits for the process to play itself out. In an attempt to democratize the process, efficiency is completely lost as the person standing at the board attempts to feverishly capture the thoughts and ideas raised in complete sentences. Before you know it, the time has run out, so the committee of decision-makers elects to go back to their huddles and come back to the group with the decision they came up with. It's more likened to totalitarianism versus democracy. Raise your hand if you've witnessed this.

Then there's, the *Demand for Solutions Only* approach. This not a process as much as it is a directive, "Don't share a problem without a solution." In other words, if a person offers a complaint or criticism about a problem without also proposing a solution, their perspective will not be considered. This is often stated in the positive, sometimes layered with toxic-positivity posters, "Complaint-free Zone," or a suggestion box in the back of the room. However it is framed, the communication is clear, one is not free to point out the elephant in the room unless they have weighed the monster, measured its girth, contacted a series of giant animal moving companies for an estimate, and have selected the best one with the best equipment and qualifications to move the monstrous beast from their midst. Then, after all of that mental labor, they have to propose it publicly, hoping that their leadership agrees with their solution or that their colleagues don't pick it apart. It's the ultimate form of risk-taking, one that has potential rejection peering at every corner. It's not just a faulty paradigm; it's stress-inducing. So, what do most people do when they see problems that they do not immediately know how to solve? They stay quiet and wait for those with power or influence to recognize it and come up with a solution for the staff to execute, whether they agree with the decision or not, returning to the faulty top-down approach. Raise your hand if you've witnessed this.

Fig 1.3 Demand for Solutions Only

The problem with all of these approaches is that they cater to the preference of authority and the ones with the loudest (or most amplified) voice. I am not only speaking out of observation, I am speaking out of the experience of being one of the outspoken, loudest voice types of people. I offer these critiques humbly, not because I believe I have all the answers, but because I understand that my actions have caused harm. I have raised my hand first, spoken the loudest, and come up with quick solutions, and with both teachers and students, I have aimed for compliance over critical thinking and collaboration. I have been very egotistical, insensitive, and inefficient. I could tell you several specific stories as examples of my missteps as a leader. All of the above examples come from different epochs in my teaching and leadership experience. When it comes to faulty problem-solving, I am legend. To any of my former students or colleagues that I have hurt, you can put your hand down now. My bad, I am trying to do better.

Previously, I had always followed a traditional approach to problem-solving that involved identifying the issue, coming up with a solution, and implementing it. However, my perspective and practice shifted when I was introduced to design thinking, a different method of problem-solving that involves more internal work and external steps. This process has helped me to approach problems in a more holistic and systematic way.

What is Design Thinking?

Instead of trying to think of solutions in isolation, or by listening to the voice of whoever speaks the loudest (or fastest), there is actually a way to take a systemized approach to identify the problem, asking the right questions of the right people, and collaboratively coming up with solutions. You may have heard of something called design thinking and heard it explained as a step-by-step approach to problem-solving. This is only partially true. First and foremost, design thinking is, well, *thinking*. It is thinking like a designer. And ultimately, what designers think about is how to creatively solve problems in ways that meet stakeholders' needs. Therefore, a designer is a creative problem-solver. So, say it with me and say it loudly, "design thinking is a mindset, not a model. If you are familiar with one design thinking model, I can introduce you to 10 others[2]

If you have ever had the privilege of having an interior designer visit your home, they may complement the decor with the statement, "I love the design choices you made." As they walk through each space, they carefully observe every surface, corner, color, and texture, seeking to understand the homeowner's preferences and evaluate them against their own personal preferences, established design principles, or current trends. They are both admiring and being critical, with the intention of suggesting solutions that fit the context of the home. They are not like an inspector, evaluating if your home is "up to code," but rather, a collaborative thought-partner, working with the limited resources at your disposal to help you make improvements that you can literally live with.

It is also important to note that every designer has preferences and biases. Those biases may be subtle in some cases, simply known as personal taste or predilections. As long as those preferences don't hurt anyone, they are benign. However, sometimes bias goes beyond personal preferences and manifests as prejudice against certain groups of people, or a lack of consideration for the potential impact of one's design on others. If design harms others, by definition, it is bad design. Sometimes the changes and modifications needed are minor. In other cases, depending on the scale of the problem, the solution is to start over completely. Some things can be revamped, other things can be restored, but in some cases, the best thing to do concerning an entity or a process or an institution should be to reimagine it completely. In many cases, that entity, process, or institution was created to solve a problem. Sometimes that original problem no longer exists. In other cases, new problems have emerged that the former solution does not address, or in some cases, that the former solution has caused. Consider the institution of public education as an example.

Historically, schools have emphasized discipline and standardization since these were qualities that factory owners desired in their workers.[3] Because of the history of the very foundation of how schools were created, there are many problems to be explored and exposed. In the context of school, the question is not whether problems exist, but rather, whether we recognize the problems and whether we will allow them to continue. Let's take for instance, a school building with many visible cracks on the exterior. These exterior signs may reveal a much bigger problem. The foundation itself may need to be repaired and all of the other things affected by this original problem- walls, floors, ceiling, etc. Based on the gravity of the overall damage, for the sake of the safety of the students and staff, a decision has to be made on whether or not it is costlier to repair the building or to move into a new building. Repairing a bad structural design will cost something. The question is, how much? Therefore, we note that a designer not only identifies the problem but begins to take inventory of the effects of the problem and then begins thinking about ways the problem could be addressed. Once you start doing that, you are thinking like a designer.

What are some problems you see in your school setting? Who do these problems affect?

Whenever I hear a presenter at a conference or seminar say, "*The* design thinking process is..." I let out a cough and say, "not the only one," in the hope that someone will ask me to explain. As previously stated, design thinking is a mindset and not a model, but for some reason, people automatically define design thinking by whatever model they are most familiar with. Too often, design thinking is defined by the process, the use of post-it notes, chart paper, markers, and specific exercises such as customer journey maps and Crazy 8's. There is nothing wrong with any of these exercises or these materials, but the reality is that none of them define design thinking. *Thinking* defines what we design.

I was introduced to the concept of design thinking in 2016 in Boulder, Colorado, as part of my Google Innovator program. If unfamiliar, Google Innovator is a global program for those seeking to bring an innovative solution to the educational community, and includes being a part of a small cohort and receiving coaching and mentoring for a year (shout out #Col16). Though undecided on what my project would be, I was laser-focused on the mission of bringing an equity-centered solution to a larger problem that existed in education. While most of my peers took notes on their digital devices, I had my colored pencils and a small notebook out, doodling mind maps to capture my thoughts and taking notes of the various guest speakers at the Google campus in Boulder. The colors seemed to capture the attention of others, asking inquisitively, "do you always take notes like that?" At this same event, a guest speaker came in to share about a process called design thinking. I remember having a brief conversation with her, and before she left, she surprised me by handing me a yellow workbook called *Design Thinking for Educators*,[4] and saying, "I just feel like you should have this." It felt like one of those serendipitous moments, where someone picks you out of a crowd and says, "I believe you have something to say, and it is time to finally say it." I honestly do not know why she gave me the book, but I am grateful that she did. For the next three years, I would immerse myself in this discipline commonly referred to as human-centered design.[5] The biggest lesson I learned that day and in the subsequent years was that if you want to effectively solve a problem that affects people, start by listening to the people the problem affects.

That little yellow book introduced me to IDEO's model of Discovery, *Interpretation*, *Ideation*, *Experimentation*, and *Evolution*.

Fig 1.4 IDEO Design Thinking model

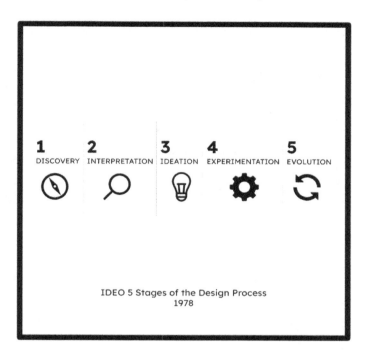

Later that year, I was in a conversation with a friend who had attended a design thinking fellowship program that introduced me to what I would later discover to be probably the most popular design thinking model for educators, by Stanford's d.school. I still recall the conversation we had over lunch when he explained that, "design thinking is human-centered design." He went on to explain that it starts with empathy, as it requires you to put yourself in the mindset of the person who will be using your product or service. "It's not about your intention, but about their expectations and desires," he said. I was sold on this model that explicitly called out empathy as the starting point. It was fleshy, less cold. It was more human.

Fig 1.5 d.school Design Thinking model

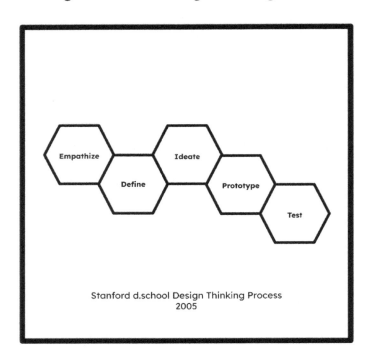

Stanford d.school Design Thinking Process
2005

I began reading and studying every resource I could find on this model of design thinking and immediately started employing it in the projects I was working on, and even taught my 4th and 5th-grade students "Every Day Is Party Time" as a mnemonic to remember, Empathize, Define, Ideate, Prototype, Test. It got laughs and giggles as I explained that this is the mantra my youngest kids, the twins, live by. They wake up ready to party, much to the chagrin of their older siblings and parents! By starting with empathy, the designer begins with people- their needs, hurt, and desire for change. My journey in design thinking was just beginning, though.

Some debate the order of steps or the emphasis of one design thinking model over another. Nevertheless, a design thinking process is simply a systematic approach to applying a designer's mindset. Applied design thinking can also be referred to as creative problem-solving. A designer is always looking to improve a situation or make something work better. A designer is always looking for flaws or gaps that exist in a particular place. A designer sees a real-world problem and questions how it can be solved. In most cases, a designer uses a combination of instinct, learned skills, and a repeatable approach to solving said problem.

But here's the thing, it is also full of bias. The designer tends to center on themselves, to make sense of something through their limited perspective. Ideation, for instance, is the most imaginative and creative step in the process that my students loved most. It's where any and all solution possibilities are imagined and captured. Out of a hundred bad ideas, one may emerge as the one to prototype and test. While practicing this exercise with my students, I noticed some limitations of this approach when trying to come up with solutions for some of the most visibly marginalized members of our community who lived right outside our windows: the homeless. What stood out was that the solutions were always limited to the ideas generated by the people in the room. Even if we did rigorous academic and empirical research, we went back into our own space and tried to develop ideas to solve problems for their space. Our experience was limited, and as a result, so was our empathy.

At a different Google Innovator event in New York City in 2019, my friend and design thinking facilitator, Les McBeth, asked, "Have you heard of Liberatory Design?" She explained it as an adaptation to the d.school's model, requiring the designer to notice their bias throughout the entire design process. So naturally, I was intrigued, and I had to learn more!

Fig 1.6 Liberatory Design

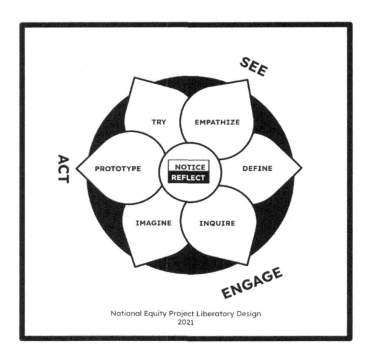

National Equity Project Liberatory Design
2021

Originally released in 2016, the Liberatory Design model was updated in 2021, and the accompanying Liberatory Design cards are a great resource to help you, "redesign power structures and institutions for liberation!" Liberatory Design (www.liberatorydesign.com) is the result of a multi-year collaboration between: Tania Anaissie, David Clifford, Susie Wise, and The National Equity Project (represented by Victor Cary and Tom Malarkey).

I'm fortunate enough to own the cards, and I've had the privilege of getting to know one of the co-designers, David Clifford, personally. What I love the most is their emphasis on mindset over and above modes or models. That is the emphasis of this book- mindset first, methodology second.

As I continued to grow in my appreciation for design thinking, I found myself using it more and more and even teaching it to my students. Since I was trying to engage younger learners with a process that was developed by design firms and graduate schools, I eventually co-developed another approach that focused on two elements: simplification of language and gamification of process. That process eventually became the end result of my Google Innovator project called, Solve in Time! The current form of the process was the result of a gradual evolution and refinement over time. I am deeply grateful to my daughter Landis for her feedback in making it enjoyable for all involved. You can read more about my project at solveintime.com/about.

Fig 1.7 Solve in Time!

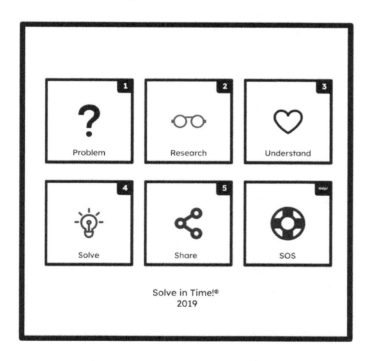

Let me be clear: this book isn't about making a choice between different models, but rather recognizing their shared elements and primary goal, which is to involve people in resolving real and relevant problems. Though much time has been spent talking about design thinking models, this is not a guide for utilizing a design thinking process. Further, this book is not about how to think like a designer in general, but rather about how to think like a designer who works to demarginalize design.

What questions arise when you view these different models?

Regardless of how it is depicted, design thinking is simply an approach to design that starts with cognitive and emotional empathy. This emphasis on empathy is more about the mindset and intentions of the designer than it is about the actual first step in the design process. From a technical perspective, Tim Brown from IDEO is correct in saying that the first step is the discovery phase, or identifying the problem itself. However, it would be inaccurate to say that the designer is the one making the discovery, just as it would be inaccurate to say that Christopher Columbus "discovered" America (since it was already inhabited). The discovery phase is simply about hearing the problem and preferences expressed by the people affected by the problem. The designer's role is to help amplify the voices of those experiencing the pain caused by the problem.

Who Designed, Design Thinking?

As already shown, Stanford University's d.school is often credited with popularizing design thinking in the education sector in the early 2000s. Others may consider the establishment of the design firm IDEO in the 1990s as the starting point for the design thinking approach. Some will look back even further and see that its origin story is hard to trace to a single individual or company, but rather a collection of ideas that have grown over time. As a sociologist and educator, I can attest that most protocols and procedures are simply iterations of previous operations rather than completely new inventions. For example, consider the creativity and engineering required to build the ancient pyramids in Egypt or Central America. See how they not only varied in size but in complexity depending on how much time and resources were dedicated to their construction. A system was created, followed, and iterated over time in those civilizations as well as many others too numerous to count. Identify an ancient civilization anywhere on the globe, and you will see problems related to communication and preservation overcome by critical thinking, creativity, and improving former systems.

For instance, in most Western societies, we may think of ways to accomplish something in a short step-by-step linear manner: steps 1-3, or steps 1-5, steps 1-10. In other cultural traditions, processes may have been expressed cyclically or even in multi-layers and dimensions. Even in education, we are quick to credit a singular "genius" instead of acknowledging the ideas that came before them that they built their ideas upon. The Western "inventor" gets credited for systematizing or codifying something that may have long existed before them. Further, those ideas are often translated and expressed in a way that makes sense to the community those ideas are being introduced to. Before there was Marzano, there was Freire. Before Carol Dweck popularized "Growth Mindset," she adapted the concept from Abraham Maslow's theories of self-actualization. Maslow, of course, popularized the hierarchy of human needs. However, few acknowledge that he co-opted it from the Niitsitapi (Blackfoot) nation and adapted them to fit his individualist ideology, which he shared with the likes of Sigmund Freud and Carl Jung. We have a doctrine of discovery problem regarding popularized codified concepts. Demarginalizing design requires us to dig deeper and acknowledge the myriads of people who have contributed to our current thinking, especially Black, Indigenous, and people of color.

Fact check time! Search "Maslow and Blackfoot."

Whether through appreciation, appropriation, or complete co-optation, the point is that rarely are "new" ideas truly original. Most ideas are built on the work of others in some way. Most design processes are a conglomerate of ideas that get popularized over time. Those who set out to operationalize design thinking have leaned on their cultural experiences to communicate how it works.

Before design thinking was popularized, there were two already well-established processes utilized by the sciences and engineering: the scientific method and the engineering process. For the record, on IDEO's website, they acknowledge, "IDEO is often credited with inventing the term design thinking and its practice. But design thinking has deep roots in a global conversation that has been unfolding for decades."[6] You see, there is something wildly western about our fascination with crowning a lone ranger, a sole proprietor, a singular achiever. There is a fine line between acknowledging someone for clearly articulating a codified process and perpetuating a colonized mindset. It's important to recognize and give credit where it is due, while also being aware of and actively working to dismantle systems of colonization and oppression.

Pause, let that breathe. How did that statement affect you?

At some point, the invention of so-called man-made products and processes are all the result of solving problems. Whether functional or aesthetic or both, at some point, someone saw a problem and tried to figure out how to fix it. Those who were successful likely looked at how systems work in nature and borrowed ideas from others that had solved adjacent problems to figure out how to tackle a new challenge. Problem-solving is never done in isolation. Problem-solving requires listening and learning, which takes time. Problem-solving requires experimenting and iterating. Design thinking may be a relatively recent term, but thinking like a designer is part of our makeup. In my cultural tradition (which includes faith), God made everything, intentionally and deliberately, to serve a purpose. He is the Creator, master designer, and inventor. And the crown jewel of his creation is humankind, made in his image and likeness and with the ability and purpose to design and create new things. But, again, this is not new. This is very ancient!

Design thinking was invented far before we can easily trace it. And whether or not you believe in a deity, most likely you believe that you were made for a purpose. And that purpose includes solving problems that you recognize around you, with those affected by those problems around you. This desire to right things that are wrong or improve things that seem not quite right is a gift we should all use to bless others. So, the question is not simply who created design thinking, but rather, what will you do with the passed-on traditions of design thinking to solve real-world problems that affect our school communities and society at large? Who will you bring along on the journey? How will you demarginalize design?

CHAPTER 2

Good Design Starts with Equity

People often speak of God being even-handed.
God is not even-handed. God is biased, in favor
of the weak, of the despised.
– Desmond Tutu

Why Begin With Equity?

If you are an educator who is familiar with design thinking, you likely believe that the process begins with the letter "E." While I agree, we may still have some differences in our views on empathy as the starting point. Though I greatly appreciate Stanford d.school's design thinking model that starts with empathy, I still have some internal conflicts as to the practicality of it all. Some designers are familiar with and concerned about the problems that plague the most marginalized. Sadly, many are not, which means the only ones that receive attention are the ones that are already the most privileged and whose concerns are already most prioritized. This is especially true when design thinking is looked at as a professional industry in which firms are paid top dollar to help businesses, organizations, and affluent schools to fix their so-called problems. When framed as a problem-solving methodology, design thinking requires the designer to define and understand the problem that needs to be solved.

My question is, is it really a problem at all? Do a quick Google search of the word "problem," and it yields this definition as the top result, "a matter or situation regarded as unwelcome or harmful and needing to be dealt with and overcome."[7] From this definition alone, we can see that there are levels to this thing we call problems.

In a 4th grade class today, there is a student being asked to solve the following so-called problem:

> Brad has 500 pieces of candy. 295 of them are red, and the rest are green. How many green pieces of candy does Brad have?

See the problem? This isn't a problem at all, it's a puzzle, and it's puzzling to me that we have not seen it as an ethical violation in our educational settings to not distinguish the two. One of these things is not the other.

For some, inconveniences of various sorts are considered "unwelcome." In many cases, these already privileged and powerful organizations are looking to increase their efficiency and optimize productivity solely for the sake of profit. Contrast that with schools in ghettoized communities inhabited by people suffering from the physical harm of unclean water, insufficient healthcare, food deserts, housing discrimination, etc. Communities that face such challenges often rely on external organizations, such as government agencies and non-profits, to advocate for their needs and develop solutions on their behalf. However, this reliance on outsiders to represent and address their problems can be problematic, as it can lead to a lack of autonomy and agency within the community. On a larger scale, the oversimplification or overgeneralization of these issues can also be problematic, as it fails to accurately capture the complexity and diversity of the problems faced by these communities. While empathy is a crucial component of a design thinking process, it can also introduce bias into the problem-solving process. On the contrary, though, if you start with equity, that is, ensuring that the voices of the most marginalized and oppressed are amplified, genuine empathy can actually be experienced. Start with empathy, and you will quite possibly miss it. Start with equity, and you will get empathy every time.

Problem-solving requires something more than a designer that takes on an empathetic mindset but an equitable one. A demarginalizing designer sees those that have been marginalized, hears their pain, and prioritizes their real and significant problems over the superfluous preferences of the already privileged. Herein lies the crux of the issue- how can someone utilize a design thinking process to solve problems for others if those others do not first express the problem to them? Or how does that person trust that their pain that has been described in various ways over various years will finally be acknowledged or addressed? How does the designer even notice the problem if the person does not share it with them, either due to lack of proximity, trust, or both? See the dilemma? Don't get me wrong, I love forcing the issue by putting empathy at the forefront of the problem-solving process, but doing so assumes that a problem has been already expressed and has been heard and valued enough to be explored deeper by someone external to the problem. To prioritize the voices of the marginalized, the first step is to be present in the same space as those most affected by the problem. Demarginalizing design requires equity.

Consider the various problems that educators aim to solve *for* students, without student input. As Gholdy Muhammad states in her critical work, *Cultivating Genius*, "There have been too many data meetings, curriculum meetings, or problem-solving meetings without students' voices at the table.[8]" Exposure to and experience with students does not equate to understanding their pain. "Putting students first" means more than educators imagining what they need, but bringing their thoughtfulness, their understanding, their literal voice to the conversation. I intentionally and unsarcastically use the term "educator" broadly to include classroom teachers, administrators, curriculum designers, tech directors, counselors, etc. We must move beyond thinking *for* the audience that is affected by a problem and begin thinking *with* them. To think *for* them is to keep their voice in the margins. Again, we must demarginalize design.

If a designer is going to make a deliberate decision to start with people as their focal point, then my one amendment would be to make sure that the most marginalized are being listened to. The designer should make a deliberate choice to listen to the ones whose voices are typically drowned out by those with more influence or social regard. If only the people who already have a voice identify the problems, then the ones without a voice never get to raise their concerns. If the most marginalized and oppressed ones have to rely on the ones with a voice to speak for them, how can they be assured that is going to happen? How can they be sure that their opinions and perspective are being properly identified if the people who are less proximate to the pain are the ones identifying it?[9] See, the dilemma is much more than simply putting people first. Rather it is to make sure the right people are being put first. If we are going to approach the design process with a mindset, then we need to ensure that mindset is equity. The problem-solving process cannot start with empathy if the "discovery" of the problem is inequitable. We have to ensure that the voices that are rarely heard are amplified. Then and only then can we hear the problem correctly and make observations and interpretations necessary to apply proposed solutions. To be explained in much more detail as you progress through this book, this is the problem with the traditional model of design thinking that I am seeking to solve.

A designer simply sees a problem and is willing to ask enough questions to see if they can solve it. SpaceX Flight Software Engineer Chen Ye defines design as "systemized problem-solving... It says, 'Hey, this thing sucks! I have a couple of ideas about how to make it better!'"[10] If this language is too crude for you or your audience, I recommend simply changing the wording to something more palatable. Instead of saying, "suck," try, "stuck". Explain design thinking as, "Hey, this thing is *stuck*! I have a couple of ideas of how to get it *unstuck*." If that works better for you, run with it. It's the same principle, just utilizing differentiated language depending on your audience. Sometimes relationships get stuck, projects get stuck, outdated processes and procedures get stuck, and often, people get stuck in the margins.

Here's the kicker, though, sometimes things are stuck from the outset. They are designed to get certain things stuck while allowing other things to flow freely. Schools are often designed to stick it to certain schools that serve certain students. Let's decode the language so we can properly identify the problem. If you ever hear or use the following descriptors: "low-income," "low-achieving," "underserved," "Title I," or "inner-city," we all know what you are saying. Just come out straight with it and say that you teach in a school that is predominantly Black and Brown. Go ahead and acknowledge that our school systems are failing these students and seem to have no idea how to properly serve them. Starting with the practice of assigning teachers who are foreign to a student's cultural upbringing and who may adopt an authoritarian role can contribute to negative perceptions of students of color. These students may be seen as lazy or defiant if they do not engage with the content or comply with the teacher's communication style. This can lead to punishment and further negative consequences for these students. It is important to recognize the impact of these cultural and power dynamics in the classroom and to work towards creating more inclusive and culturally responsive learning environments that support the success and well-being of all students.

Tracking gets them stuck on a trajectory towards classes that suppress their voice and agency, pushing them to comply with hard and fast rules, do busy work, and be punished if they do not conform to the norms of that context. Their punishment may start with a referral in pre-school, which turns into a folder that is filled with a collection of notes including detentions and suspensions, somewhere in there the student is diagnosed and given IEP, culturally biased tests begin in the 3rd grade on content the kid never cared about, dropout rates increase, petty crimes turn into harsh sentencing, and the pre-school to prison pipeline is perpetuated. In one sense, they are stuck in a downward cycle. But if it is running freely, is it really stuck, or is it performing as designed?

Suppose one aims to solve the problems that affect the white middle-class community. In that case, the argument could be made that the incentive for solving these problems includes lowering crime rates or stopping wasting tax dollars on recovery programs or prisons. In fact, that was the approach to President Obama's My Brother's Keeper Initiative. Unfortunately, the entire whitepaper was framed from the outset as an investment opportunity by the rich and middle class for their long-term financial gain. See the problem? A program for Black and Brown boys is centered on whites and the well-off. This is why empathy by itself is not a sufficient enough motivator for change. If the system has been working successfully for my gain, why should I care about others? It's like deep down, the staffers knew that to make their program appealing to the general public and worth the investment of supporters, the problem had to be shifted from the young men adversely affected by centuries worth of systemic oppression to the long-term profitability of the potential investors. Some would say that this was just clever marketing. Indeed, Heather McGhee's book, *The Sum of Us*, speaks directly to the fallible idea that we live in a zero-sum society, where the idea of sacrificing for another means losing something for yourself.[11] Not only is this untrue financially, but it is also most untrue morally and ethically. I would argue that it was a significant compromise of values. It was a value shift that was purposely made to appeal to the mindset of the people that could help solve the problem through their financial support and emotional support. As long as the people with power and control saw their own gain as primary, they would not block it (or allow it to get stuck). I'm not saying that it was an unwise move or inherently faulty, as much as I'm saying that it is frustrating that the primary motivating factor for helping the marginalized is not out of moral obligation but a financial one. It's a frustrating reality that people who can intervene in situations for others require them to be convinced that there is something in it for them. Therefore, I will continue to argue that design thinking cannot simply start with a mindset of empathy. There are too many mental and emotional blocks for some to prioritize the upliftment of others. Empathy is a choice that centers on your ability to have compassion for others. To make the process effective for all, it needs to be more equitable. For problem-solving to be effective for the people that are "stuck," it needs to start with another E. It must start with *equity*.

What is Equity?

I understand terms are hard to keep up with, and standard definitions do not always help. Look up the definition of equity in any standard dictionary, and you will likely find yourself less clear than when you began your inquiry. Merriam Webster, Cambridge, Dictionary.com, you name it, they all get it wrong. Look it up for yourself, but for the most part, they all define equity as having to do with fairness and impartiality. As Dr. Tatum states when talking about a different social justice term, "Who wrote the dictionary?... Whose interests are served by [that] definition?" [12] If equity is defined loosely and irresponsibly as "impartiality," then it loses its meaning. Equity is hard to understand and even harder to explain. I get it. Personally, I like to use the example of a 400-meter race as an illustration of equity. I ran track as a youth, and after being enamored with the sport starting in 1984 when the Summer Olympics were hosted just a couple of miles away from where I was raised in Los Angeles, California. It was my absolute joy to watch the Tokyo 2020 Olympics with my children and see their fascination with different sports, and certain athletes grow. Two big questions came from my children (ages 14, 11, and 10 at the time) as we watched the Games. The first is, why was it called the 2020 Olympics when it was the year 2021? The second was when the Women's 400-meter race started, and my children began asking questions about how the runners were staggered in their lanes. One of my daughters asked with sincerity in her eyes as she pointed at the screen, "why is that runner all the way out there" pointing to the person in the outside lane, "while this runner is all the way down there?" pointing to the runner starting in the inside lane. "Yeah, I was thinking the same thing!" her sibling exclaimed. What would proceed was a conversation about equity versus equality.

Fig 2.1 Equity Looks Like Staggered Lanes

Equity Looks Like Staggered Lanes

I explained to my children that if they all started at the same position, then the person in the inside lane is at an advantage because all of the other runners have a longer distance to run around the track. When you look at the whole oval, the closer you are to the inside of the track, the less distance you have to run. I explained that the 400-meter dash illustrates equity, as opposed to equality. For those highly invested in the concept of meritocracy, the common complaint is that equity initiatives such as affirmative action are unfair because they worked hard to get where they are, not realizing or admitting that they were always given the inside lane on a non-staggered track. Conversations about the need for additional funding, support services, strategic hiring of teachers of color, and so forth in an attempt to consider the long arch of history of disqualifying Black and Brown people from even competing in the race of the so-called "American Dream." Yes, these are regular conversations in the Lanier household!

I had the privilege of being in the room at the Google offices in Sunnyvale, California, in 2017 when Dr. Jeffery Andrade gave one of the most dynamic talks I have ever heard. The title of his keynote was *Equality or Equity: Which One Will You Feed?*[13] I distinctly remember his explanation of the distinction of the terms by telling a hilarious story about his twin sons. One son, Taiyari, is thirsty. His other son, Amauru, is "hella thirsty." To give them both an equal amount of water would seem reasonable, but the problem is that Amauru will likely still be thirsty. While sitting in the audience, I laughed probably louder than I should have, partially because I'm a father of twins myself and knew it to be entirely accurate. My son is Silas, and my daughter is Ellis. Between the two, there are hella differences! Silas was always hella hungry when they were babies, whereas Ellis was a picky eater. Nowadays, Silas is often the first person awake in our house, but Ellis can sleep hella long. See what I mean? To give both the same exact amount of food, sleep, etc., would not result in equitable outcomes. If I give Silas the same amount of food as Ellis, his needs would be underserved. Give Ellis the same amount as Silas, resulting in waste. So obviously, the correct response would be to take inventory of their differing needs and distribute those resources accordingly.

Obviously, this is an analogy comparing the families and students that are advantaged and disadvantaged we serve in our educational system. When trying to figure out what is "right and fair" for each child, the first question to ask is, "why are there hella differences between the two?" My point is to look through a lens of equity, one must also have a lens of compassion. To look at any situation without both lenses in your optics is to not see the situation clearly. Equity requires empathy, and genuine empathy requires equity. Equality, in many cases, is unfair. Compassion is complex. Compassion comes at a higher cost to those far removed from systemic, institutional, historical, and contemporary forms of inequity. Yes, I am speaking about race, class, and gender (just to name a few). The reality is that our educational system has never been set up equally. To make up for that difference requires filling in holes that exist for some that have never existed for others. To do so runs the risk of being called the very thing you are attempting to not be- unfair, biased, or, my personal favorite (sarcasm), someone practicing "reverse-discrimination." To reverse something that causes harm is to put its effects in reverse. That takes deliberate action, not inaction (think climate change, trauma, substance abuse, etc.). To truly make things fair in our so-called meritocracy, we have to stagger the lanes.

Herein lies the problem with simply aiming for equality instead of equity. By definition, equality is impartial. On the other hand, equity is purposefully partial to those with higher levels of need. Equality would say that the person in the ER with a skin rash gets treated before a person with a broken bone because it would be "fair and impartial" to treat the person with the skin rash. After all, they were there first, right? Equity demands that we triage the person with the more severe injury. Or like the real-life instance where I was told by a college professor that I could not make up a midterm that I missed while I was away at my cousin's funeral because it would be "unfair to the other students." Yes, that really happened. No matter how objective we attempt to be, fairness has always been a subjective matter. The question is, how are we employing empathy as part of our efforts in being equitable?

Equity requires the work of needs assessment and distributing resources according to need. As it pertains to technology in education, for instance, giving each child a laptop to take home to complete homework may seem fair because the same resource was distributed evenly (and without partiality). A more equitable approach would be to take a needs assessment of the technology that already exists in your students' homes and distribute technology based on the difference in need. One student may not get a laptop, while another may get a laptop and a hotspot. Another student may not need a laptop or a hotspot because they have adequate technology at home already. Though the state may give a school an equal amount of funding for technology per student, the school may distribute those limited resources differently based on the results of their needs assessment. The first challenge is coming up with a plan to properly assess the technology needs of each student. Plain and simple, equity requires more work by those responsible for distributing resources. If we are to design with equity in mind, we must see what our students and families need, aim to meet those needs, and set our class expectations based on our knowledge of any existing inequities. To see with proper vision, you must look at every student and every family through the lens of equity, and in doing so, you will be able to properly apply empathy.

Fig 2.2 Key Characteristics of a Demarginalizing Designer

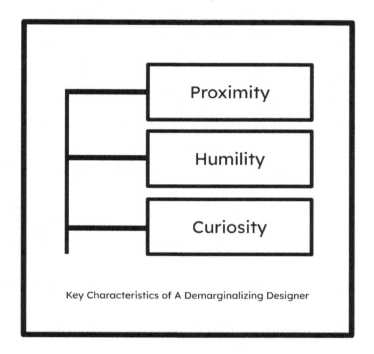

Key Characteristics of A Demarginalizing Designer

How Is Equity Aligned with Empathy?

What if I told you that whatever you have highlighted or written in the margins of this book says more about you than the book itself? Look around and see all of the other words that are printed. Why did you leave all of those words unmarked? Is it really because all of the other words were unimportant, or was it because something in what was written made you want to remember it or to debate it? What caught your interest was possibly a confirmation of your bias or a challenge to it. Whether conscious or unconscious, we all see what we are not only able to see but what we want to see. This is why we must open our aperture wider, adjusting our eyes to accept what may be similar or opposite of what we think to be obvious. In doing so, we challenge our own biases.

At the end of class one day, while a student voluntarily began organizing the class tablets back in the charging station, I asked him to stay after for a few minutes so we could talk. I recall looking him in the eyes and saying something to the effect of, "Tate, I have to confess something to you. I saw you differently at the beginning of the school year than I see you now. Multiple teachers warned me that you were "trouble" and that I should be prepared to have a conflict with you in my class. I was wrong to listen to them, and I was wrong to believe them. You're an amazing young man. It's been a pleasure teaching you. I'm sorry. Do you forgive me?" He just gave me a wry look and nodded his head. Our relationship continued to grow from there. What did I do, exactly, that was equitable and empathetic? First, I acknowledged my impaired vision, i.e., my bias, which was influenced by external sources. Secondly, I started allowing Tate to speak for himself. As I did this, I started seeing him as the highly complex, intelligent, sometimes conflicted person that he is. I began to empathize with his imperfections. I began to see myself in him.

The ultimate exercise in humility is to acknowledge that we all have biases. If you automatically read that I called you a name, like short-sighted, prejudiced, or something more heinous, like, bigoted, take a deep breath, hear what was stated versus what was not. Instead of taking offense, it is important to define what the word bias means. As previously stated, standard definitions can often be unhelpful. My good friend Ken Shelton gave me the heads up that Collins Dictionary typically offers better definitions for social justice terms, so that is a source I often reference. Collins defines bias as "a tendency to prefer one person or thing to another and favor that person or thing."[14] See, I didn't call you names. I simply said that you have preferences, but I would warn that those preferences can be dangerous if you are in any position of power and your actions based on your preferences negatively affect others.

If you are a teacher or an admin, you are in a position of authority over others. In that position, you have the opportunity to listen and learn from the people in your care. With them, you can co-design a "forever getting better" experience based on the collective knowledge in the room. You can build buy-in to whatever decisions need to be made because you co-design the solutions instead of coercing your team to adopt your plan. To get there, though, you must make sure that you co-identify the problems that hinder the children and adults that you serve. To do that, you must give more weight to their preferences and less to your own. To give weight to their preferences, you must hear from them. You must yield the floor and listen and learn what problems exist, how those problems affect them, and potentially where the source of the problem lies.

If you are in a position of power, your words and your opinions carry a certain level of gravity. People tend to acquiesce to the opinions of their leaders, again, often due to unconscious bias- or fear. As Liberatory Design advocates in their mindset cards, they implore the people that problem-solve to work to transform power, namely, by exploring "structures and opportunities for interactions in which power is shared, not exercised."[15] Consider any working group or committee you have recently been a part of. More often than not, the person who does the most talking is crowned the group's de facto leader. The person with the most decisive opinion (regardless of the breadth of experience or education), or the person who seems most passionate about the topic, gives them the distinctive honor of being distinguished as the leader of any said discussion group. Here's the question, though, are they actually the most qualified simply because they are the most outspoken? The real question is, should they be talking at all? Instead of voicing their opinions first, leaders stop, listen, ask more questions, and seek to hear instead of being heard. As I often say when coaching leadership teams, those with the most weight should *wait*.

This is where ego has to be put aside because a teacher, team leader, or administrator must be willing to hear that they are potentially a part of the problem. Demarginalizing design requires recognizing that we are all potentially a part of the problem. Further, we are all potentially a part of the solution. Instead of taking offense, the leader should be encouraged as they recognize that not only has the problem been properly identified, but that they are also the ones that can intentionally share their power to bring about necessary change. If design thinking is truly being utilized, the desire to satisfy the needs of the client- the parent that sent the angry email, the staff member that only has something negative to say, the student that belts aloud, "this is boring" - those are the people you are called to serve. Their problems are your problems. Instead of countering their complaints and wielding your power to exert force, a designer who is committed to equity leans in and asks questions. The people that bring the complaint are the ones most qualified to tell you what's painful, what's hurtful, and what's antithetical to the mission and vision of the school. My advice, listen to them, listen closely, and most importantly, invite them to help redesign the solution. This is how you empower the marginalized.

In listening to the complaints of others, you are taking inventory of their perspective. The best thing you can do at that point is to assess the size and scope of the problem by asking others. The call is not to listen to "the balanced" viewpoints of everyone but to listen intently to the people that communicated the problem. Listen to the people most proximate to the pain. If the problems that plague our school systems were systematically orchestrated by the same people that are pontificating on how to solve them, then they need to be hit with the "with all due respect" disclaimer and politely told to hush it. If the person who is doing the most talking is adjacent to the pain of it, then they need to do their best Aaron Burr impersonation- talk less, smile more.

However it needs to be communicated for them to hear it, the perpetrators of the problem need to be reminded that they may not be the most qualified to describe the problem because they do not personally relate to it. If they can only see the problem from their vantage point- statistics that point to dropout rates or failure rates or discipline rates- and their language itself communicates a need to create more structures or more discipline, or more accountability, then they have self-identified as the least understanding and the least compassionate of the realities of the students they claim they aim to serve. If a person is so confident in their beliefs that they express them with an authoritative voice, rather than humbly, then it's important to challenge those views. The best way to do this is to encourage them to learn from different perspectives and truly engage in the educational process. It is only through this that everyone can benefit from a truly equitable learning environment. The reality is Black and Brown students make up the majority of the students in schools in American cities are being served by a predominately white workforce. These educators live in predominantly white neighborhoods and hold extremely different values and perspectives than the very students they are charged with the tall task of caring for.[16] Dr. Christopher Emdin describes our many Black and Brown students as "neoindengionous," meaning the people that most identify with the indigenous people of this colonized land that some other people's forefathers claimed as their own.[17] Much like the Standing Rock Sioux people were the ones most qualified to speak up and call the Dakota pipeline problematic to their community, your Black and Brown students are the ones most qualified to speak up against the construction of the prison pipeline perpetuated by our school systems. If you are not native to the people affected by the problem, your duty is to become an anthropologist of those most proximate to the pain.

The first step in this exercise is to self-reflect to identify your primary role in the design thinking process. Ask, "On what levels do I identify with the students I am in charge of caring for?" Let's start by decoding the language that is so often used to describe school demographics to level with the reality of what we're really talking about. If your school is described as mostly disadvantaged, under-resourced, underserved, or urban, we all know what you are talking about! Make it plain. You are likely describing a school populated by mostly Black and Brown students who come from households that are close to or below the poverty line. Other social markers to consider include gender, language, and culture. If you find yourself adjacent to the people experiencing the effects of the problem, then your job is to listen and listen well. Here's the rule, "if you can't relate, don't pontificate!" Instead, position yourself as the lead listener.

The people that are furthest away from the pain of the problem identified should be clamoring to take on two roles in a design thinking process- note-taker and researcher. This is not intended to silence their voices or minimize their opinion, but to intentionally turn the volume down on their voice and turn up the volume of the people that need to be heard, metaphorically speaking. If you look at your team and realize that you do not have representation of voice at the table, you may have identified a bigger problem, or quite possibly the source of the problem! Representation matters because without it, your entire process is inequitable. Some would call it rigged. The perspectives of those that understand the problem best are relegated to the sidelines awaiting the sympathy of those in power to give them the basic resources necessary to meet the standards of expectations that others have set. If they are not at the table of decision-making, i.e., problem-solving, then your design thinking process is all for naught. If you have less proximity to the pain of the problems of the very community you serve, then you are not only viewed as an outsider by them; you must see yourself as an actual outsider to them. This is not inherently bad, it is inherently a reality that needs to be leveled with.

There is a predictable next step that many will take that I feel needs to be addressed, and that is to invite more representation to your table of decision-making. It is a somewhat well-intentioned but potentially harmful solution to the problem. The very idea of inviting someone to your table is to acknowledge your authority- something else that makes you less proximate to those in pain. If you have the authority to invite them in, it also means that you have the power to dismiss them, whether literally or figuratively. The social dynamics of a tokenized Black teacher being invited to the comfortable space of mostly white admin is an intimidating and toxic environment. The pressure on that person to share their opinions without fear of retribution, let alone the need to code-switch to speak your language, the many microaggressions endured, and the mental calculus necessary to evaluate what is worth challenging versus not is an exhausting exercise. If you have not been in that sort of setting where fear and worry abound because you know that your every move and word is being judged, you should put yourself in an environment where the power dynamics are clearly not in your favor. As Emdin suggests in his TED talk, *Teach Teachers to Create Magic*, you need to get out of your comfort zone and start visiting the hood.[18]

White educators, it is past time for you to visit the Black barbershop, the Black church, the hip hop cyphers on the block where the power structures look and sound and feel much different than what you're used to. When you realize that the loudest ones talking are just expressing themselves, where the shouts are both Amens and cries of anguish. Where if you're not dressed to impress then you may get clowned, but if you dress with too much finesse, then you may get jacked. If you don't know what clowned or jacked means, stick around for a while and the vernacular will make sense as you immerse yourself in the cultural context where others are in charge. The hood is where you learn that the term "clown" is slang for being made fun of, and your dignity is diminished if you don't know the code of the streets where the weak are broken, liquor is poured, and antidepressants run rampant because the pain is deep. Where you might see the young man with aggression in his eyes and in his tone of voice yet how his entire countenance is shifted once an older Black woman walks by. The Black elders are respected here.[19] They are the most revered simply because they survived the very streets young Black and Brown girls and boys are currently navigating. There's a code that still exists in the streets, respect your elders. "Pull up your pants!" "Yes ma'am."

This swapping of power structures is what sociologists refer to as social interactionism. You may be highly regarded with lots of prestige in your school setting, but in someone else's hood, you're a stranger, needing to ask for directions, while also intimidated and afraid that you may break some unwritten rule that can be detrimental to your safety. That feeling of lostness and worry is likened to what your students feel when they enter your space, where the rules are set by you and others like you. If you don't have older Black women on your staff who are affectionately known as mothers in the community or the younger men and women who are mentors to the kids charged under your care, you need to know where to find them. It's time for you to be outnumbered at the table, so the deliberate action of elevating equity may increase your empathy. The person most qualified to identify the problem is the person who most identifies with the problem. Listen to them. Learn from them.

Listen to the Black and Brown people that are expressing the problem, they are the ones that are experiencing it. Another way to say it is to give preference to the people most proximate to the pain. Those are the people most qualified to tell you more, to build your understanding of the gravity and complexity of the problem. No matter your preferred design thinking model - this is the discovery phase; this is the empathy stage. Be encouraged! The initial complaint is what you need to hear to begin the process of problem-solving. Because you are prioritizing the people with the complaint, you are listening intently, taking notes, and maybe unbeknownst to them, you are already recruiting them to be a part of the problem-solving process as you begin to ask more questions. This is equity put into practice. This is demarginalizing design.

CHAPTER 3

Becoming a Demarginalizing Designer

Be Humble
– Kendrick Lamar

Where Are Your Blind Spots?

In English class in my 10th-grade year, I used to stare at a sign under the teacher's lectern that haunts me to this day. It stated, "I am not who I think I am. I am not what you think I am. I am what I think, you think I am." The attribution was anonymous, and the message was perplexing. This quote affirms what I referred to earlier as Social Interactionism, which in short is a concept that explains that we navigate the world hoping others see us in a certain way so we can get what we want. We are self-centered in that way, aiming to maneuver through different contexts and situations, vying for the respect we need to get what we want. We use whatever clout we have as cosmetics to cover up who we really are in favor of persuading others to perceive us in a certain way. Unfortunately, others respond to the social norms that are in place and either give us the respect we desire or fail to give us the respect we deserve. We live in a highly inequitable society, some living in the stress of attempting to climb the social hierarchy, or others simply living in it and not having to be burdened with over-contemplating the privileges afforded them. To truly empathize with those that are external to them, the demarginalizing designer needs to develop an attitude of deep humility. This deep humility is nurtured through intense self-reflection, which is necessary if we are ever to be properly equipped to see the needs of others. The attitude of deep humility acknowledges that we all have blemishes, most notably, biases that block our ability to see the most marginalized people in our midst and to elevate their voices above our own.

This sort of deep humility is only accomplished through self-reflection. Who are you? Who are you really? How do you self-identify? It was a personal exercise in humility when a webinar host requested that I write out my personal pronouns on a slide. I have followed the lead of others in naming my gender pronouns (he/him/his), but the actual exercise in going deeper to share how I self-identify also gave me deep humility in understanding that I possess many social advantages and disadvantages depending on my context that I do not regularly acknowledge. I am more than a Black man in America. Looking in the mirror, I am a Black Christian male, straight, married, father, native English speaker, natural-born US citizen, and so many more privileges to name or count. There's a lot to unpack in that reality. Still, the biggest takeaway for me to reflect on is the biases I may have due to my personal identity and experience within the context of the United States of America in the 21st century. Deep humility recognizes that I do not inherently understand or identify with those of a different race, faith, gender, social status, or a long list of other things if I am honest enough and courageous enough to acknowledge. My age, social status, background, the things that I have seen, and the beliefs that I have all make up the parts of who I am. Seeing the unique perspectives and honoring the perspectives of others is absolutely critical if I am to be of any service to them. But first, I must start by reflecting on who I am.

Fig 3.1 Sample self-reflection questions

1. **Who** do you present yourself as to others?
2. **What** are your deepest personal values?
3. **Where** were your values developed?
4. **When** were they developed?
5. **Why** are they important to you?
6. **How** have your values changed over time?

To deepen your understanding of self, it is imperative that you reflect on your personal bias that may be blocking your ability to fully see others around you. For example, when in the hallways or the cafeteria, whose attire and hairstyles do you most frequently notice and why? Teachers in the classroom, do you pay more attention to and take offense to the Black young men in the back that are laughing loudly but do not notice the white young ladies in the front that are giggling and passing notes? Do you hear a loud sigh and look to see who made it and interpret it as blatant disrespect if it came from one person and not another? Are you more gentle or assertive in tone depending on the identity of the students and staff that whom you interact with? Do you think they notice that you are not always kind and that they are not blind to the preferences you give because what comes from your lips is often switched depending on who is the recipient? Let me offer to you that others may notice what you do not; your opportunity is to examine your bias, so your credibility is built over time.

A starting place for recognizing your blind spots is to take an implicit bias test from Harvard to identify your personal biases concerning race, gender, sexual orientation, and other topics.[20] The knowledge of those biases deepens your humility and allows you to see where you may have the internal prioritization to listen to one group over another. Bias tends not to see things as they are, but as you imagine them. Your bias is revealed when you prioritize the voice of those you have an affinity with and ignore the need to make sure you listen more intently to the ones you don't understand. Your understanding and recognition of personal bias will help you recognize opportunities to be intentional with your conversations and listen more intently to those traditionally you would be less likely to consider or acknowledge. If you aim to be culturally relevant in your instruction, you must be adamant about recognizing your cultural bias.

Furthermore, if you have gathered the people most proximate to the painful effects of whatever problem you aim to solve, and if trust and open communication are present, they will be your most adamant supporters by telling you when they notice your bias. That trust can be built by obnoxiously asking them often to point out your blind spots. If you are in a position of power based on title or otherwise, your requests for critique may have to be reiterated and repeated so frequently that the people that answer to you are fully convinced that you truly value it and have no intention of using it against them. Hear this warning, do not ask for feedback if you are unwilling to listen and learn from it. To quote a friend, "Feedback is about growth, not compliments." For better or worse, you must reiterate that you give them permission to analyze your words and actions and how they impact others. A humble leader is a humble learner, one who learns to listen to those they may otherwise overlook. Asking others to point out what makes them feel uncomfortable, what makes them less vocal, and what causes them to pause from sharing their full, unbridled opinions may let you know whether or not you are getting the most from the people that surround you.

Deep humility is absolutely necessary for connecting with those in a different position than you and those that are culturally different than you. In her acclaimed work, *The Dreamkeepers: Successful Teachers of African American Children*, Gloria Ladson-Billings states that teachers that adhere to culturally relevant practices have two main qualities: high self-esteem and high regard for others.[21] High self-esteem can withstand critique because it is rooted in humility and not a false form of high self-esteem or arrogance. High regard for others is displayed through consistent interaction and inquiry into what they see as your strengths as well as your flaws. Humility doesn't just give them permission or demands that they share, but that they understand that they actually have the power and the agency to inform you of your bias in ways that are most comfortable to them.

How often has an admin or a teacher made a ridiculing comment after they have heard critical feedback, "It has just come to my attention that some of you have been complaining about…"? Instead of introspecting and possibly hearing that they have not created the conditions for critical feedback, they take offense that their decisions are being questioned or how dissatisfaction is being expressed. Have you ever examined how you expect others to communicate the problems they are experiencing? Are the means of communication systems you have set up for yourself, or were they collaboratively created by the people you hope to hear from? When they share their problems with a decision you have made, do you take personal offense and feel tempted to remind people of your authority, or do you honestly and adamantly thank them and lean in to hear more of their perspective? When others express dissatisfaction with something you have communicated or had a hand in creating that affects them, a person with deep humility expresses gratitude because those dissenting voices actually grant you valuable insight into how to see beyond your bias and how to design a better design experience for them moving forward.

The goal of deep humility is to simply learn what biases may be blocking your vision from seeing what they need to see. In other words, it is to get out of the way, so the real problems that affect people can be seen properly, and the people who are affected by those problems can be given the full attention they deserve.

Who Do You Need to Hear From?

If you are in a safe space, literally and figuratively, I invite you to try the following mindful exercise by scanning the QR code below. If you are in an area where you feel comfortable, close your eyes, sit comfortably with your back straight, feet flat on the floor, and hands in your lap. Breathing through your nose, focus on your breath moving in and out of your body. If physical sensations or thoughts interrupt your meditation, note the experience and then return your focus to your breath.

Fig 3.2 Whose Voice Do You Need to Hear?

Whose Voice Do You Need to Hear?

Congratulations, you just experienced a design thinking exercise. You may not have solved the problem yet, but hopefully, you now know where to start, that is, who to start with. It starts with the people the problem affects the most. Not just imagining them but gathering them.

Unfortunately, some leaders call others to be brave in their attitudes and actions, while they display the least vulnerability in the room. Somewhere along the way, these leaders have bought into the notion that vulnerability is a sign of weakness or that a leader's call is to display strength and personal adequacy at all times. This can prove detrimental to the rest of a working team because problems are downplayed, and blame is shifted to circumstances or other people. Instead, when leaders acknowledge their own shortcomings and look through the lens of deep humility, they invite their entire team to the same mental and emotional place- not to give up, but to feel the problem deep enough to commit to the creativity necessary to solve it. Problems are felt, failures are real, and when our bias is not blocking our ability to listen intently, the question can be asked with humility, "what is wrong with our current design that is producing these sorts of results?"

Further, they realize that a leadership committee is incapable of answering "what is wrong" on their own. Deep humility elevates equity by reminding the designer that they have a lot to learn from others who are different. In other words, the demarginalizing designer asks, "whose voice is missing from the room?" If the people most proximate to the pain of the problem are missing, then whatever efforts to solve it are all for naught. If the problem is poor professional development for teachers, for instance, then the teachers should be gathered and asked what good professional development looks like. If the problem is related to parent communication, parents should be in the room to explain more and share how the communication can be improved. By looking closely at who is involved in the decision-making process in schools and opening the doors to the rooms that have traditionally been closed to those most affected by the painful effects of the problems schools create and perpetuate, the empathetic shift moves from simply caring about people to actually caring for them.

Researcher and culturally responsive educational theorist Geneva Gay makes the distinction between caring "about" versus caring "for" by stating, "'caring for' is deliberate and purposeful action plus emotionality."[22] If the most prominent and consistent problems plaguing the school are related to student learning, student discipline, and student nutrition, guess whose voice is most obviously needed? Way too often, teachers and faculty gather in their huddles, trying to improve the social and emotional well-being of students, the attitudes and behaviors of students, and the engagement and outcomes of students but are missing the most critical voices in the conversation. If you realize that you have not been building equity by elevating the voices of those most proximate to the pain experienced in school, then to quote the *Substitute Teacher* from Key & Peele, "You done messed up!" Thankfully the fix moving forward requires just one thing- gather the people most proximate to the pain and give them voice not only to share more but to be engaged in coming up with solutions.

I am fully aware that "I done messed up" plenty of times, even recently. Because I was conditioned in the culture of education, I have made it my personal mission to grow in my competence and to display my expertise at all times. To this day, I struggle with going too far down the line in developing a plan to solve a problem that affects others without gathering and listening to those very people most proximate to it. I know this to be true but often fail to exercise the humility of putting understanding before planning. Because I am no longer a full-time classroom teacher, most of my time is dedicated to listening to instructional coaches and school leaders describe the problems they perceive their teachers and students are feeling. I recently worked with a colleague as we planned a series of professional development sessions to support a school district that was feeling the pains of remote learning amidst the COVID-19 pandemic. I led the way in consulting with the leaders, analyzed data provided by them, listened intently to the desires of the admin, and came up with a professional development plan to meet those goals with their teachers. Did you catch the problem with this approach?

It humbles me to admit that I know better than not listening and prioritizing the people most proximate to the pain. Instead of meeting with the teachers and asking, "what do you need?"

We went to the administration and asked, "what do you think they need?" We were not elevating the voices of the hurting to hear their pain points. We did not ask the right questions of the right people. After reading the survey results of our first couple of training sessions with the teachers, we obviously missed the mark majorly. We asked for critical feedback, and that's exactly what we got! The feedback was brutally honest, and as the one responsible for the planning, it was definitely my fault. I pre-designed a plan versus collaboratively creating one with the people most proximate to the pain. The teachers did not see the relevance of professional development to the challenges they were experiencing, and thankfully, they did not hold back from telling us. To connect to the teachers' feelings, we needed to enter the space with enough humility to listen to what they were saying. So instead of rejecting any of the comments as disrespectful or just "focusing on the positive," we went through the painful process of filtering the feedback to focus on the harshest words for us to absorb. After sifting through painful expressions such as "waste of time" and "I don't see the value in this," we kept reading for the *why* behind their critiques.

What these teachers were begging for was simply more time. We learned that on top of the stresses of the pandemic, the need to learn new technology, and the need to apply new strategies, their planning time was replaced with professional development. We were piling on to the already overwhelming and overburdening them with more strategies without giving them the space and time to actually strategize. When my colleague and I looked over the survey responses and focused on those experiencing frustration due to the so-called solution we were offering, we finally started to experience the empathy we were pursuing. Setting aside our assumptions and our pride, we dug deep with a learner's mindset asking, "what don't we know?" and "what don't we yet understand?" We had to acknowledge that hurting people sometimes say hurtful things. The pain they expressed may have been harsh, but they said it loud enough for us to finally hear it and for their admin to hear it as well.

Fig 3.3 Investigative questions to ask

1. **Whose** voice is missing from the conversation?
2. **What** do they think about this problem?
3. **How** do we know?

How Curious Are You?

When a situation is delicate, or the stakes are high, the common refrain is to proceed with caution. Caution is good if it acknowledges that real people are affected by real problems, and our supposed solutions can cause further damage. That awareness is crucial, but there is also a drawback of proceeding with so much caution that it stifles creativity. A demarginalizing designer must proceed with an *insatiable* curiosity to balance this reality. Like an investigator looking for clues with a magnifying glass in hand, this sort of designer proceeds with curious questions, wanting to learn what they admittedly do not know or understand. The teacher or the admin that is deeply humbled by their own bias does all they can to listen intently to the people most affected by the problem and positions themselves as the most curious learner in the room. Asking questions to learn what is unknown is how curiosity is cultivated. Curiosity is more than a character trait; it is the exercise of asking questions like "why" with the same annoying frequency as a two-year-old trying to understand their world for the first time. A well-skilled problem solver has an extreme desire to discover what they do not know, so they ask more questions and are convinced that the answers are there, if only they continue to ask the right questions of the right people. From this position of humility, the demarginalizing designer's imagination and creativity grows as their understanding of the problem and the people affected by it grows.

Teachers and admin are to become anthropologists of the people who are plagued by the problems they aim to solve. Asking questions is clearly the most effective way to gather information about the people you aim to serve. The demarginalizing designer is aware that the people affected by the problem, the people most proximate to the pain, understand it better than anyone else. The designer asks them as many questions as possible to gain insight and understanding from them. A process that any curious learner can employ to gather unknown information is the same set of questions I was introduced to as a 7th-grade social studies student. Every week, we were assigned to find a current event article and fill in the blanks to the ever-familiar 5Ws and an H outline: *Who, What, When, Where, Why,* and *How.*

I recall using this same set of question-asking and information-gathering processes as a reading comprehension strategy for SAT prep and later research studies in grad school. I have found this process helpful for making sure any form of literature is properly interpreted before being acted upon. I have used it for years as a classroom teacher and in my instructional coaching strategies. The goal is to gather as much information as possible to properly interpret the situation before offering your opinion. If you do not make proper observations, you will not properly interpret the situation, leading to an improper application or action. In other words, you cannot solve a problem that you do not understand, and you cannot understand unless you first ask the people that know the most about the problem you hope to solve.

You may be wondering, how many questions should you ask in the information gathering process? My question in return is, how curious are you? A general rule that can be applied in many situations is the concept of "Three Before Me." This rule is mainly used as a research and collaboration technique by teachers to ensure their students refer to three sources of information before asking the teacher for help. It's masterful, and I use it all the time! Another way to apply it conversationally is to ask three curious questions before responding. In other words, what three questions are most relevant to ask before offering any form of suggestion? I call it the rule of "Three Questions Before Suggestion." In my role as an "experience design coach," I frequently listen to people describe challenges that I do not fully understand. Admittedly, it is easier for me to apply curiosity to subjects and situations I have the least familiarity with. For example, if I meet with a math teacher or a Special Ed instructor, I am immediately cognitively and emotionally aware that I have more to learn than offer. What comes next are the good ol' fashioned 5Ws and H questions, fishing for the information needed simply to understand the situation better. It is actually a fun internal challenge to ask myself, what are at least three different types of who, what, when, where, why, or how questions do I need the answers to better understand this situation? The real challenge is maintaining an insatiable curiosity in situations that I think I already understand. The Three Before Me rule applies in all situations, not just the ones I immediately find most puzzling. Remember, the demarginalizing designer is to remain deeply humble, so, therefore, all assumptions are put to the side in favor of discovering unknown or even surprising answers. Problems must be properly identified to be properly responded to.

The demarginalizing designer possesses an insatiable curiosity to discover the actual problem and not the one they presume to be the issue. They ask open-ended who, what, when, where, why, and how questions in such a way as to get out of the way of the learning. Instead of interjecting their opinions that can often override or stand in opposition to the people's opinions most proximate to the pain of the situation, they stay humble and stay hungry. This is a patient and sometimes painful process. Nonetheless, it is the best course of action to define the actual problem. Alternatively, when closed-ended questions are asked, the conversation often comes to an immediate halt. For example, if the designer asks, "So are you saying that the problem is ...?" The response is limited to either a yes, no, or a correction! For the person experiencing the pain to be best positioned to help solve it, they have to understand and articulate it for themselves. The designer allows them to process their experience and express it on their own.

Further, the designer avoids injecting their own experience into the problem identification phase. Though it is tempting to connect with someone else's situation with "I remember when I faced a similar situation," the result is the conversation shifting from the person who is experiencing the problem to the person interviewing them. If they want to know your opinion or ability to relate to their circumstance, they will ask; no need to interject. To focus on the problem is to focus on the one experiencing it. The designer never positions themselves in front of the person sharing their pain. They are alongside them, offering them a supportive ear. They are behind them, willing to take their lead, but they are not in front of them, pulling them where they think they should go.

Sometimes in the question-asking process, it is apparent that the root of the problem is still not completely understood even though it has been stated. Another form of question asking that the designer may use to understand the heart of the issue more deeply is to use the "5 Whys" or 5Y Technique. Because this form of question asking can feel unnatural or forced, I highly encourage telling the person or people you are interviewing that you are about to engage in an activity that involves asking the same five questions in succession to discover the potential root of the problem. Instead of trying to mask it as normal conversation, just name it, "This is a protocol called the '5 Whys', in which I will ask you the same question multiple times. It may seem awkward or obnoxious, I know, but are you ok with me asking you these questions?"

Fig 3.4 Five Whys Sample Situation

The cafeteria worker has complained that he needs more help to help the lines move faster, but the school admin has stated that the staff all have other duties during lunch and that they do not have the budget to pay for more workers.

The admin has put it on the cafeteria staff to "figure it out" and the cafeteria staff has made a request that has been rejected.

It seems like this situation will simply go unsolved unless alternative solutions that do not involve more resources are offered.

Why is it a problem that the lines are backed up?

If we don't have more people working in the cafeteria, then the lunch lines will continue to be backed up and this will continue to be a problem.

Why is that a problem?

It's because I do not have enough people here to help. They won't pay for help, and they won't give me any teachers to assist either.

Why is that a problem?

Because it all falls on me. I cannot move the lines any faster when some kids don't remember their lunch ID or some kids don't have enough money on their balance, or some kids have to wait for change.

Why is that a problem?

Look, some of these kids aren't eating lunch because they don't have enough time, and the teachers tell them to clean off their trays and to get back to class. It's just not right!

> **Why** is that a problem?

> *Because some kids are not eating food! I watch some kids not even get in line because they know they don't have enough time to eat. Teachers just come in to pick up the kids to take them back to class and fuss at them for talking, but I see what really happens. The kids don't have time to eat!*

Finally, the problem was uncovered. The students do not have time to eat. The solution may be to increase the number of workers, but there are other solutions to that problem that have yet to be explored. Before, the problem was focused on the school resources. Now the problem is centered on who is experiencing the pain the most- the students. Restated, the problem is, "students do not have enough time to eat lunch."

Based on the example above, whose voice needs to be heard?

Curious questions not only drive conversation, but they are a catalyst for compassion. Open-ended questions innately communicate interest in others. Even more so, when it is known that questions are being asked to help and not harm when they are a part of what the designer sees as the discovery phase or aspect of empathy, then the person being asked questions is being interviewed and not interrogated. In this process, the designer has collected more information to better understand and connect to the people experiencing pain. This is designing with equity in mind. Additionally, bringing those people directly into the problem-solving process is what we call demarginalizing design.

Part II

An invitation continued- Share your thoughts using
#DemarginalizingDesign @deelanier on Twitter or interact with Dee
and others in the following Flip group:

flip.com/DemarginalizingDesign

CHAPTER 4

Battling Bias

Don't Believe the Hype!
– Flavor Flav

What About Collective Bias?

I love sociology. Ironically enough, my first sociology class was titled "Sociology for Non-Majors" with Dr. Harry Edwards at UC Berkeley in 1995. I took it as a prerequisite course to get my breadth requirements out of the way, not knowing that I would fall in love with it and pursue it further even though I had no idea what I could do with a degree in the field. Instead, I ended up earning not just one degree majoring in sociology, but two! And though I loathed the unclear path it set me on, sociology shapes how I read the world. In an attempt to explain what a sociologist is, I often describe it as a professional that attempts to understand the thinking of the masses. A psychologist is to the individual, as a sociologist is to groups of people. As a result of thinking like a sociologist, I find it important to stress that individuals can do all they want to recognize and battle their own personal bias but may find their opinions and actions swayed when in the company of others. It's what the social sciences dub collective bias, or groupthink phenomenon.

Simply put, collective bias is how others influence us in making decisions as a group. It's what it looks like to roll with the flow because it's not worth being the only member of a group that dissents. It looks like being told, "that's just the way we've always done things around here." It looks like being isolated or attacked if you continue to push against or disturb the tradition of a particular practice (including the practice of simply agreeing with certain people in positions of authority). But, of course, organizational bias gets more complicated, or in some cases even dangerous, if there is no dissenting voice. Think, the 1921 Tulsa massacre. Think, the 1994 published book, The Bell Curve, passed out to Congress members and laws created based on its bogus data. Deep down those lawmakers believed there must be validity to the idea of Black intellectual inferiority.[23] Think, 2021 Capitol Hill insurrectionists. Collective bias is implicit bias on steroids. It endures through time, counter-research, and in some cases, counter-common sense. It pushes false narratives and feeds off FUD (fear, uncertainty, and doubt) simply because of its strength in numbers.

"It's just the way things are done around here" is the death knell to any meaningful dialogue about anything that may require change. When that statement is made, it is like a line drawn in the sand that reads, "This is our culture, and these are our traditions, don't cross this line." It's like a child asking their parent, "why?" only to be responded to with the gauntlet of all parental comebacks, "Because I told you so!" In the case of tradition in school culture, saying something to the effect of, "this is the way things are done around here," is worse than your momma saying because I told you so. It's worse than your momma and your daddy told you because we told you so. It's worse than your momma, your daddy, your grandma, your auntie, and all your cousins and 'em saying because we told you so. It's like every living relative, your dead homies, and your ancestors rising from the distant shores of your native land to collectively tell you, "Just go with the flow and stop asking so many dang questions!" Obviously, this could be related to school policies, classroom practices, parent communication, and after-school activities. To proverbially pushback requires bravery, authority, or both. This is mainly because an individual is going up against collective thought, not just another individual.

Nonetheless, meaningful change, especially school and classroom culture, cannot be attained without meaningful dialogue with those most proximate to the pain. Not only does the demarginalizing designer need to maintain deep humility and insatiable curiosity, but so does the entire school community. The janitor, the after-school program coordinator, the counselor, the assistant principal, the dean, the art specialist, the cafeteria worker, the reading specialist... errbody! The institution of education needs to be freed from the effects of bias prevalent in every facet of education, including school nutrition, grading policies, standardized testing, disciplinary actions, curriculum standards, tracking, and so much more. For the institution to change, everyone involved must contribute their collective thought, but most importantly, they must listen to the voices of those in the margins. I was recently contacted by a group that hosts annual conferences for students, and they asked if I could lead a session on design thinking, "Since you are the expert," they said. I had to correct the statement outright and immediately, "No, the students are the experts." The sooner we invert our perspective to believe that the ones who feel the pain of their experience are the experts on solving it, the better. Sure, they could use a guide or facilitator to capture their thoughts, but the actual expertise lies with them. Ask them curious questions like why, where, when, and how. Ask the same sort of questions with deep humility to the teachers who are gasping for air due to constantly inhaling the toxic fumes from putting out figurative fires in their classrooms while also bearing the load of expectations from administration and parents. The people who are hurting the most are experts in what pain feels like, which makes them most qualified in offering solutions on how to mitigate it. When you sense pain, make it your goal to lean in and listen.

Teachers and admin, look around your school buildings and consider what practices are normative or performative without clear relevance to the students. Interrogate the policies that students complain about the most and research whether or not their existence promotes emotional or academic success (Yes, I put it in that order on purpose). Let me mention a few that I have noticed in my teaching and coaching career. Starting with some of the things other teachers and I were expected to produce and make visible, supposedly for the students, but clearly as adherence to some mandates and traditions without clarity of connection to student comprehension. Here are my top five practices in school that, in many cases, I felt the pressure to conform to due to collective culture, but made no sense to me:

- Punitive discipline techniques (like taking away recess time for bad behavior)
- Teaching to the test (standardized tests, specifically)
- Confusing multipoint rubrics (written on the level of the teacher and not the student)
- Unimodal Instruction (meaning, only allowing for one way to learn)
- Bulletin boards (yeah, I said it)

Some of you may look at this list and feel a bit confused, but whether they cause you to react with, "Huh?" or "Hmm?"

"Ahem!" or "Amen!" My question to you is, what would be on your list and why? What research and logic have been made manifest in an attempt to clarify and validate the existence of certain policies or procedures that everyone is expected to blindly adhere to? When you were in college, what educational theory do you remember being introduced concerning assessment practices, homework policies, classroom design, daily procedures, grading, attendance, punctuality, etc.? Some of us learned radical things in early childhood development and physiology classes, such as the effect of sunlight and color and movement on the brain. The connection between creative expression and content comprehension. We learned the advantages of proper nutrition and sleep and physical activity. Still, it seems like schools are more interested in test-taking strategies to overcome so-called achievement gaps than any of these. Many teachers start their careers ready to be the change-makers, the perpetual cycle breakers, only beaten down within their first few years by a mentor, an administrator, a collective of other teachers that have learned that it's simply easier to comply than to continue to ask questions such as, "Why?"

Where Do You See Bias Hiding?

As the saying goes, you cannot control others; you can only control yourself. Nonetheless, you can at least be aware of your personal contribution to collective bias. See the list of definitions on the following pages as a starting point. Just a starting point. If you look at this list and want to exclaim, "But what about (fill in the blank)?" I feel you, fam. Bias is much bigger than this starter list. Write the many more you know of in the margins, @ me on social media, and wake me up to the reality of realms I have yet to experience. Demand an updated edition, a more complete compilation, call a senator to take note and act, a dismantling and then a demolishing of some of the lighter and darker forms of discrimination, from the unconscious to the unconscionable. If this list leads you to act, then I've done my job. Consider yourself provoked.

Fig 4.1 Examples of Bias

Dunning-Kruger Effect[24]

Dunning-Kruger Effect is a cognitive bias in which people wrongly overestimate their knowledge or ability in a specific area. This tends to occur because a lack of self-awareness prevents them from accurately assessing their own skills.

Bandwagon Effect[25]

Bandwagon Effect is the tendency for people in social and sometimes political situations to align themselves with the majority opinion and do or believe things because many other people appear to be doing or believing the same.

Confirmation Bias[26]

Confirmation Bias is the tendency of people to favor information that confirms their existing beliefs or hypotheses. It happens when a person gives more weight to evidence that confirms their beliefs and undervalues evidence that could disprove it.

Halo Effect[27]

Halo Effect is a cognitive bias that occurs when an initial positive judgment about a person unconsciously colors the perception of the individual as a whole.

Ingroup Bias[28]

Ingroup Bias or ingroup favoritism is the tendency to respond more positively to people from our ingroups (group of people with a shared interest or identity) than we do to people from outgroups.

Choice Supportive[29]

Choice Supportive is the tendency to remember our choices as better than they actually were, because we tend to over-attribute positive features to options we chose and negative features to options not chosen.

If these terms are new to you know they are not likely new to your environment. If you consider yourself a demarginalizing designer or at least aspire to be one, never forget the prerequisites of deep humility and insatiable curiosity. Please note I'm also speaking to myself. When I observe this list, I have anecdote after anecdote, story after story of how power and privilege have conspired to jade my perspective on what's happening all around me. Nonetheless, nothing helps you sort through your own emotions or external accusations of paranoia than a tall glass of good old-fashioned, hard-cold facts. I'm talking stats, figures, bar graphs, pie charts, we're talking, data! If the year 2020 taught us anything, it reminded us that facts and figures are not the quick fixes to cognitive dissonance, but they can at least help.

So whether or not you have a boss who postures themselves as all-wise and all-knowing (Dunning-Kruger effect) and people tend to take in all of their untested theories due to their charismatic personality (possibly halo-effect), or because they can relate to their identity marker (ingroup bias), everyone simply following along, even if you have doubts (bandwagon-effect), and the collective attitude of never looking back at the previous decisions made (choice-supportive) you don't need to know any of these terms to come to terms with the fact that you have contributed to what we call collective bias. So the goal is to discover what data will help you break this cycle. Looking at the research in advance of decisions being made or dissecting the data on the outcome of previously made decisions should free you to make better decisions in the future. Why does this matter? Because… students.

Right now, you may be expecting me to hit you up with a bunch of facts, some national averages, and longitudinal studies that will blow your mind. But I'm not going to do that. Instead, I would like to lead you on an even deeper exercise in humility. I triple-dog-dare you to go on a data mining scavenger hunt to discover these data points in your school or district.

Fig 4.2 Data Scavenger Hunt

What percentage of your Black or Brown students have been...	
placed in gifted and talented programs?	
placed in special education programs?	
placed in honors or AP classes?	
suspended annually?	

What other questions do you now have? Now with those figures in tow, how in the world do bulletin boards help dismantle and demolish these inequities? If they don't increase student imagination and don't disrupt disparity, then why do we do it at all? That would be my challenge to any school that focuses on perpetuating traditions rather than alleviating inequities in education.

Who Is Being Hurt By Your Bias?

Out of the sample problems related to bias, the one that stands out to me is the problem of confirmation bias. In lay terms, Confirmation bias is what happens when your prejudice encounters a congruent example. It's the stereotype that all Black people are good dancers and seeing a group of Black teens stepping during recess and thinking, "See, they are just naturally good at that." Unfortunately, the stereotypes don't end at dancing or athletic ability. Do me a favor and do a search for the statement, "Black male stereotypes." What do you notice? What do you wonder? Now take the exercise deeper and discover how many of those stereotypes are positive and have nothing to do with physical attributes or ability. See where I'm going with this? I am a Black male, so this is personal to me. I see overwhelming evidence that society sees me as more threatening than intelligent, more probable to be angry than passionate, and more likely to be criminal than competent.

I recall an instance in which I was carrying an armload of iPads to a classroom, and the principal of school stopped me and asked, "Hey, what are you doing?" I knew what the real deal was. I knew that he wasn't asking out of curiosity and that his inquiry wasn't without suspicion. I also knew not to show my offense and look at him with the same cold look he was giving me. I knew better because I am consciously aware of the stereotypes that follow me, no matter my academic achievements, my attire, or my vernacular. I was aware that I was undergoing profiling at the moment, even though my job entailed moving technology devices from one room to another. I was the tech integration coach at the school. He hired me for this exact position! Nonetheless, a Black man carrying 22 iPads down the hall after hours "looks suspicious," and at the moment, I fit the description of the type of person that would more likely be stealing than doing their job. Guess what? He fit the description in my head of the type to ask such a question and deny that it was racially motivated. He was a white male in a position of power. I was defensive based on my suspicion of him. I interpreted his questions as an in-hall inquisition. He confirmed my bias. Confirmation bias messes with us all. As physiology professor, Dr. Raymond S. Nickerson describes it, confirmation bias is a *ubiquitous phenomenon in many guises.*[30] That's why I would like to solve it.

Need to spot your bias? See this list I've dubbed, The Bias Big Four:

Fig 4.3 Bias Big Four

Bias Big Four:

1. **Avoiding** objective facts.
2. **Misinterpreting** information in a way that only supports existing beliefs.
3. **Ignoring** information that challenges existing beliefs.
4. **Remembering** details that only uphold existing beliefs.

I attended a workshop once, and an analogy was given that I thoroughly appreciate. The example goes like this. If you visited a lake and noticed multiple dead and dying fish, you wouldn't ask, "What's wrong with these fish?" Instead, you would naturally conclude that there must be something wrong with the water. But when it comes to poor people, we tend to blame individuals for their decisions instead of taking a critical look at the environment they are surviving in. I feel very frustrated by this, especially as others have attempted to use me as an example of confirmation bias. I have been spotlighted and tokenized way too frequently as an example of what hard work and determination can get you- out of the hood, into a good career, on a path to long-term success. Because I happen to break the mold entirely by providence, many ignore the fact that there are more mediocre men and women thriving in our current system of education and economy than there are incredibly resilient, hard-working, boot-strap pulling people in our larger society. Again, the focus on the micro always comes at the expense of the macro. When one chooses to squint their figurative eyes to see the exceptions instead of the rules of society, they tend to do so for the sake of proving their already preconceived notions. So, if you want to know how I really feel when someone uses me as evidence of their bias against others within my community, I feel angered and offended. When I hear a white person tell their story that they only got where they are based on hard work and without hand-me-downs, I feel like they don't understand how our society as currently constructed works. I feel frustrated that these narratives live on because people seize every opportunity to prove their own success based purely on merit and their bias against others due to laziness or inferiority. I hate that they refuse to look at the big picture and see systems at play and not just individuals operating within a so-called fair and equal society.

When doing this equitable design work, I stress the significance of being specific in your responses to questions. Answers like "I don't know" or "everyone," or "all the time" are not specific enough to create change. They do not hold anyone accountable. They do not encourage deeper investigation or action-planning. Instead, they statically sit while bias leads to policies that systematically perpetuate inequities. We need real people with real timelines and real examples of when real things occur to truly combat our biases. When I think about the issue of confirmation bias and the people that can help overcome them,

I consider the people in charge of policy creation in a school setting as the most capable of creating immediate change. However, I also recognize that if they are the ones with the most glaring bias, the ones that see things in a particular way and only search for evidence that confirms their beliefs, they are the problem that needs to be changed! These people need to undergo some form of bias analysis and be introduced to debiasing strategies. Or if they are resistant to change, they need to be replaced before they cause further harm.

To solve such problems, I need two types of people: Within the organization, give me the people most passionate about solving said problem. Secondly, and most importantly, give me people most proximate to the pain to help solve it. If they are missing from my midst, then that is the problem. We start there.

How Might You Solve Implicit Bias in Your Setting?

CHAPTER 5

Defeating Discrimination

[I]n times of crisis the wise build bridges,
while the foolish build barriers.
– T'Challa

Why Does Representation Matter?

It was February 16th, 2018, and I was preparing to give a keynote at the American School in Costa Rica in just a few hours, but I was horribly distracted. As my colleagues and I ate breakfast and talked through the conference logistics, I kept checking social media and scrolling through pics from the previous day. While wearing a Black Panther t-shirt underneath my blazer, a coworker noticed and inquired if I intended to watch the movie. In response, I gave a facial expression that conveyed my incredulity at the question and indicated that, without a doubt, I would be watching the movie. I had been on Instagram and Twitter all morning scrolling through images of friends and family donning African attire and celebrating in movie theaters packed with all Black and Brown faces. A couple of friends of mine, one Ghanaian and another Nigerian, posed with their arms crossed and their heads up, with the caption, #WakandaForever. There was something marvelous happening in the US, and it would soon become a global phenomenon. Singing, dancing, Wakanda saluting was happening wherever

Black people gathered to watch a movie that would become a box office hit, Academy nominated Best Picture, and what I have called "the cinematic diadem of the diaspora." The answer to the question was an obvious yes, I had every intention of watching the film! My wife was present with me as well, and she had already done the work to find out if the movie would be in English or subtitled, show times, dinner plans for before, the whole nine. We were ready! Though I was keynoting that morning and had several workshops that I was leading throughout the day, it was very apparent that the highlight of my day was the world premiere of Black Panther, or Patera Negra, as my e-ticket said. It was then that my coworker commented, "I am not really into comics, but I keep hearing about this movie. Help me understand. Do you think I would like it?" My eyes opened wide and what came out of my mouth was a passionate plea for understanding the social significance of such a film. It went something like this:

> First of all, this is much bigger than a superhero film. This film is a cultural phenomenon. There are a few popular Black superheroes on TV and in movies right now- look at Black Lightning on The CW network, Luke Cage on Netflix, or Miles Morales as the new Spiderman, all great examples of representation and relevance to Black people and people of color. But most Black superheroes are heroes of the hood. Black Panther is something altogether different. The protagonist is T'Challa, King of Wakanda! He is the son of T'Chaka and Queen Ramonda. His sister is Shuri, a warrior princess and science and technology genius. The Wakandan people have never been enslaved, their land has never been exploited, as a people, they have never been co-opted or controlled, and they have the means to defend themselves against any enemy invasion and

provide for all of their needs. They are an independent nation marked by royalty. They know their heritage, ancestry, accomplishments, and abilities. And they look like me!

I wanted her to recognize the deeper significance of the film. I want the same for you. On further reflection, it is the reason why I stand on stage and share at schools the responsibility of all educators to get more proximate to the pain of the Black and Brown students they are responsible for educating. If your leadership and teachers are predominantly white and your students are predominantly Black and Brown, then it must be acknowledged that there is a gap between the cultural perspectives of teachers and students that is significant enough to be explored rather than ignored.[31] Instead of positioning themselves as experts, many educators should posture themselves as humble learners of the students, and the communities they aim to serve. By simply asking a question such as, "Why was this movie so significant to you?" The lessons from the movie Black Panther are another opportunity for these teachers to understand a people from a foreign land and why outside influence is often feared. Many teachers are entering a foreign land; they are foreigners in the students' land. They are the outside influence and bring centuries of paternalistic rule under the guise of salvation. Understanding the real fear that exists not only between teachers and students but even amongst staff requires getting proximate and asking curious questions with humility.

The pain felt from cultural appropriation, where some white teachers who attempt to relate to circumstances they have never experienced say things like, "I know what you're sayin'," knowing full well that they do not. Just because you are familiar with the vernacular you hear and attempt to conform by dropping the "g" in a sentence when you speak (sayin', playin', swayin'), that doesn't mean that you have any idea of the pain that a student feels when a "G" has been dropped in the streets. I used to watch the news anxiously every morning, hoping that a reported shooting didn't involve one of my students. On several occasions, I recall coming to school and seeing students huddled up talking, some wiping away tears, only to discover that the murder of a young teen reported the night before was the sibling, cousin, or family friend. A small portrait of the slain pinned to their school uniform cardigans, with the words, "May you rest in peace," the deceased, barely a teen. When violence erupts, or a loved one is lost, I knew that my students were going to be too distracted and burdened to discuss whatever was our planned content of the day. The key point is not only to adjust your language but to adjust your entire perspective and lessons, if necessary.

It came as no surprise why there was mourning in many classrooms the day it was announced Chadwick Boseman had died. It was only after his passing that many of us learned that he had a terminal illness that he hid from the public to deliver the movie Black Panther and other masterpiece performances. The same man who overcame countless obstacles of racial discrimination was also masking his cancer and his treatments because he also knew that we lived in an ableist society that may have told him what he couldn't do instead of what he would ultimately prove that he could do. In many ways, the death of Boseman felt similar to my sophomore year in college when Tupac Shakur passed. Or when Kobe and Gianna Bryant crashed tragically on a Southern California mountainside on a Sunday morning. These people may be just entertainers to many, but they are our heroes. These people represent our culture, experience, and desire to attain what they had or at least displayed for a moment on our screens. Yet, in their lives, we saw a different reality, a royalty that harkens back to our native land before it was destroyed by foreign invasion and colonization. Do you get that kind of pain?

It is only in getting proximate to the perspective of the people that have experienced deep hurt that the educator can understand their need to be responsive to students in their current situation. Equipped with deep humility and an insatiable curiosity, the demarginalizing designer considers how they interact with the people they should be focused on learning from instead of forcing them to conform to the social and cultural norms of their historical oppressors. As Dr. Gloria Ladson-Billings states, "The notion of 'cultural relevance' moves beyond language to include other aspects of student and school culture. Thus, culturally relevant teaching uses student culture to maintain it and transcend the negative effects of the dominant culture."[32] Being culturally responsive as educators involves discovering what is relevant to our students and staff that have cultural differences and integrating those relevant issues in all that we do. In other words, we find out what others care about, introspect to see where we can find any form of mutual understanding, and collectively aim to solve the problems that plague us as a diverse community.

If we look deeply at the narrative and themes that arose in Wakanda, we see many of the same issues that affect Africa and the Americas, and beyond. Their fictional problems mirror our real-world realities. Taking our cues from the film's narrative, we can actually identify issues that our students and staff genuinely care about- and invite them to help solve them. Spoiler alert, if you have not seen the film yet, I am about to give away some of the movie's themes. I am about to give away some of the themes of one of the highest-grossing films and one of the most culturally significant movies in history. Don't worry, the main subplot will not be given away, but the question must be asked, why have you not seen Black Panther yet?! If you work in a school setting with a significant portion of your student population represented by Black and Brown students and you have not watched the movie, Black Panther, please put down this book immediately and go to whatever streaming service you need to make it happen. Your cultural competency depends on understanding the complex issues highlighted in that film. Yes, a "superhero" film is *that* significant!

What Forms of Inequity Do You Recognize?

Watch the movie Black Panther, and you will realize that many of the problems exposed throughout the narrative include a litany of *isms* or various forms of prejudice and discrimination. Isms are a way of describing any attitude, action, or institutional structure that oppresses a person or group because of their target group.[33] To quote Dr. Tatum, "The thread and threat of violence runs through all of the isms."[34] Whichever continent you live on, you will likely see that these problems are far from fictional if you look at our own society today. They are real, and they need to be combated! Here's a curious question, though- how, if at all, do you see these isms within your own school setting? What policies or practices are similar to the following terms that may expose a culture of toxicity within your school community?

Fig 5.1 Examples of Discrimination

Ageism[35]

Ageism is discrimination against people on the grounds of age; specifically, discrimination elderly people.

Sexism[36]

Sexism is the belief that the members of one sex, usually women, are less intelligent or less capable than those of the other sex and need not be treated equally. It is also the behaviour which is the result of this belief.

Classism[37]

Classism is differential treatment based on social class or perceived social class. Classism is the systematic oppression of subordinated class groups to advantage and strengthen the dominant class groups.

Racism[38]

Racism is the belief that people of some races are inferior to others, and the behaviour which is the result of this belief. Racism also refers to the aspects of a society which prevent people of some racial groups from having the same privileges and opportunities as people from other races.

Ableism[39]

Ableism is a set of beliefs or practices that devalue and discriminate against people with physical, intellectual, or psychiatric disabilities and often rests on the assumption that disabled people need to be 'fixed' in one form or the other.

Colonialism[40]

Colonialism is the practice by which a powerful country directly controls less powerful countries and uses their resources to increase its own power and wealth.

On a personal level when I reflect on my career in the classroom and later in administration, I cannot help but think of the visceral ways in which I experienced racism and the invisible ways I benefited from the presence of sexism and ageism. They stand out as noticeable when I concentrate on them, yet what stands out the most is how I began my teaching career with a colonialist mindset. My early teaching reflected the same strict, regimented, sage on-the-stage pedagogical practices I despised as a student. If you walked in the door of my classroom in my early teaching career, you would see me lecturing instead of facilitating instruction, me teaching in a didactic manner instead of giving students agency, tapping the shoulders of students to keep their heads up instead of creating interactive activities for them to engage in. You would see me telling students to study terms and master concepts with little regard for translating its importance to their context or connecting to their long-term success. I was simply emulating my own educational experience examples, unaware that I was perpetuating the problem. I am confident that I am not alone in personally being guilty of the very things I want to combat. This was T'Challa's revelation as well (If you don't know what I mean, again, go watch the movie).

On a macro level, when we consider our educational arrogance in the United States, we fail to see our peril in only comparing ourselves to ourselves. We do not look at how we rank on a global scale, not for competitive purposes, but for the sake of mutual learning from those that may have similar problems.[41] Furthermore, many do not aim to deeply understand the rich and complex diversity of our international colleagues, parents, and students. Because many lack cultural understanding, we operate without compassion or curiosity rooted in humility. When more affluent schools set up service-learning projects, it is with a colonizer's mindset, looking at "those people" that need your help to translate the language and the customs that already exist within the outside community so they can be transformed into a more successful and civilized community. Of course, there are exceptions, but service-learning partnerships are rarely established as intentionally reciprocal relationships. Instead, many of these efforts to "serve" others are an acts of self-aggrandization and saviorism. We can sometimes arrogantly believe that we can solve their problems by donating our services instead of learning how we can jointly share resources to combat the challenges that collectively plague us both.

All of these thoughts came simply from a reflection on the problems of Wakanda and how they are merely a reflection of our own nationalistic, regional, or cultural pride. Because we position ourselves as competitors to other schools, even those in our same zip codes, we deal with our problems in isolation, whether the families live in the same community, siblings attend neighboring schools or school staff commute from their "safe" neighborhoods.

What other isms are obvious that exist in your school setting? What other obstacles exist that limit your students and staff from feeling fully safe and cared for in the environment they spend at least 7 hours a day, 5 days a week, 180 days a year. We all want to learn to happen in the classroom, but we first need to recognize what are the culturally complex challenges that hinder learning for some students, including the emotional safety of the staff that is responsible for caring for the children. After reviewing the list of terms prompted from the movie Black Panther, what stands out as missing from this list? Perhaps xenophobia, which could be considered a form of racism, or homophobia, which could be seen as a type of sexism, or other prejudices? Though a fictional film, the movie Black Panther can serve as a large mirror to expose our community-wide biases and challenges worth overcoming. Using a cross-cultural connection point such as a movie as a starting point, the designer realizes that the marginalized's pain and frustration must be exposed, evaluated, and dealt with to create the conditions for effective problem-solving. When there is a room full of people who do not trust one another or understand one another, or care for one another, then problems of various sorts persist and are perpetuated by those who have the prerogative to do so. But when the community understands that exposing challenges is essential to the health and growth of the community and dedicates the time and energy to solve them, then that community is genuinely creating a safe place for all to thrive by demarginalizing design.

It's time to get specific. Out of the list of isms supplied or thought of on your own, which do you see most prevalent in your school setting? In what ways has the issue hindered your success or the success of those around you? Tougher question- in what ways have you benefited from the existence of whatever ism came to mind? Let's pause here and allow you to use the margins on the side as a personal reflection space.

Remember that the work of a demarginalizing designer is to embrace deep humility, so return to the question: what are your blind spots? Whose voices are you more partial to listening to, and whose voices are you more inclined to dismiss? Are you listening to the older staff member who states that she feels ageism is at play in the digital age where teachers are told to "get on board or see the door"? When examining your classrooms' gender, racial and socioeconomic makeup, who do you more readily identify with? Do you more readily identify with specific groups of students? What do you do to understand

and get to know the students outside of that group or groups? Looking outward, you may recognize what cultural groups are underrepresented by your board of directors. It's possible that many of your teachers profess to be "colorblind," meaning they don't discriminate based on race, but they may not be aware of the disparities in their disciplinary practices. Possibly your PTA is composed of mostly upper-class individuals who have the dispensable time to make it to meetings in the middle of the day, not noticing that classism is at play. My imagination is limited to only the types of things I have seen from my vantage point in the schools I have worked with. Still, the question is, what problems do your students, staff, board, parents, and other stakeholders see as prevalent within your context? It is worth taking the time to listen to them, dig deep to identify the present problems, and take a microscope to understand their complexity.

Your humility reminds you that you do not see everything that you should see or that you could see. If people have told you that a problem is more significant than you see or understand, your goal is to lean in and learn more. No school leader, teacher, paraprofessional, parent, or person, in general, wants to be told that there are extreme inequities in their setting. They especially do not want to be told that they may be partly responsible for the continuing inequity that exists. The reality is that we do not enjoy the pre-work to problem-solving. It feels like an indictment, like receiving a report card with bad grades or checking your bank account and learning that you have significantly overdrawn. Humility reminds us that this is also just the beginning, the starting point, not the end. Your curiosity is what pushes you forward. Your deep interest in the problems and the people they affect drives you to learn more. This is an expression of passion, a commitment to considering solutions by discovering what is at the heart of the problem and what types of solutions the community may be able to unlock if you work collaboratively with them. If you dare to proceed to understand the issues of inequity in your community, begin by bringing in the people affected by a particular problem and asking questions to understand it better."[42]

How Might You Solve Such Inequities?

For a problem-solving activity to prove effective, the most significant challenge is identifying its most pervasive presence in a particular setting and naming it. For the sake of identifying a single example, let's say that you and a small group of staff identify a bias against male students in school discipline as the main problem they would like to collectively solve.

With sexism in school discipline as the focus point, it is easy enough to report how each person has seen the inequity at play, but it takes a little work to actually look at the direct reports from the school. A small team of problem solvers may dig into the data like you did earlier and see the referral rates and the severity of consequences administered to males versus female students in their school, in their district, and how they compare to nationwide statistics. In this discovery process, one of the group members may discover that research suggests that academically disengaged black male students account for the majority of most suspensions in schools across the US.[43] Looking at the data, they not only see the consistency with national results with their own school, but a possible root cause is lack of academic engagement due to noninclusive curricula, racial biases, and poor relationships with teachers. Through research, their focus has narrowed, with a clearer picture of the pervasive problem in their own community.

Armed with clarity of the specific problem and the people that need to be involved in the solution proposal, the group realizes that they need to bring the most marginalized people to the table. The question becomes, how can they collect those voices to hear more of them? Instead of gathering simple anecdotal evidence by a few interviews, the group begins brainstorming how to collect stories from all Black male students using a school-wide survey. The purpose of the survey is to collect stories of multiple ways Black boys have experienced less tolerance from teachers for appearing disinterested in the classroom content. Furthermore, they realize they need to survey the teachers to discover why they disproportionately write discipline referrals for Black male students compared to other demographic groups. Lastly, they realize they need to help teachers integrate better culturally responsive instructional practices to reduce academic disengagement, which is the potential cause of the discipline issues in the first place.

If you were a member of this group, and this is the solution you have come up with, how would you creatively communicate it to the rest of your school staff?

CHAPTER 6

Eradicating Racism

For our struggle is not against flesh and blood, but against
the rulers, against the authorities, against the powers of
this dark world and against the spiritual forces of evil in
the heavenly realms.
– Ephesians 6:12, NIV

What Is This Thing We Call Race?

Warning, some of what I have to say in this chapter is frightening. At the time of this writing, my wife and I had just finished watching season one of HBO's Lovecraft Country, and I have to admit that I found it more disturbing than entertaining. If you are unfamiliar with the show, know that it is a sci-fi-horror series set in the 1950s where the main character, a Black man named Atticus, ventures on a road trip through the South in search of his father. He is accompanied by his girlfriend Letitia and his uncle, George, and what they encounter is nothing short of terrifying. It wasn't frightening because of the monsters, ghouls, warlocks, and whatnots. It was terrifying because buried under the veneer of blood and horror was a recounting of the realities of racism in America. At least with the scenes that were obviously science fiction, I could remind myself that it was just a TV show and not reality. But as it pertains to the harassment, the police brutality, the reality of sundown towns, and the slaughter of real Black bodies (simply for being Black bodies), I was truly terrified. It reminded me of why many people don't like to talk about racism in America but rather keep it buried in the past. If we look in the mirror, turn off the lights, and say its name too many times, like Candyman, the monster will be set loose to murder our pride.

Racist acts are not tales from the crypt; these are true accounts of horrific injustice. Many of the same people that were alive when four little girls were bombed in Birmingham, who saw Bull Connor release dogs and batons and fire hoses on children, today lay witness to the bodies of Black and Brown people being abused on the news too many times to keep count. When does the terror end? My mother was just ten years old when the Voting Rights Act of 1965 was signed, but in 2020 she and her son, her grandchildren, and the world all witnessed the calculated attack on urban districts in battleground states in the presidential election. For many in America and across the globe, speaking about racism is taboo, but if you're scared to talk about the truth, then everything we believe about education is a lie. What is the purpose of education? No matter how someone answers that question, that purpose cannot be achieved or realized without confronting our individual and collectively shared demons and shortcomings. Institutionalized racism is this country's most heinous violation of human dignity. No one is educated, in any sense of the word, without acknowledging and understanding that. The ghosts of our past leave us aghast while media outlets and politicians gaslight us into believing that talking about racism is a racist act. I believe we must still look humbly in the mirrors and curiously investigate the scene- even if the house is haunted.

I have made it a point to never talk about racism without first talking about its predecessor, the source of its power– *race*. For many, race is a given, but racism is an atrocity that must be eradicated. Racism is an issue that has plagued our society for far too long. Though we have made great strides in recent years to combat racism, there are still many areas where it still exists. But as Ta-Nehisi Coates declared in his book *Between the World and Me*, "Race is the child of racism, not the father."[44] This simple yet powerful statement speaks volumes about how race does not exist without first having been created by racist ideologies and systems of oppression throughout history. Race was created at a time for the distinct purpose of justifying a system of class. We have mastered a racialized caste system in America (read Isabel Wilkerson's, *Caste*).[45] Therefore, racism cannot be discussed without demystifying the concept of race. As seen in the previous chapter, race is a type of ism, an othering, a schism or distinction created concerning this thing called race. But because race was invented and is not actual or factual, race itself is a confounding topic. As Rhonda V. Magee describes in her work, *The Inner Work of Racial Justice*, the western world is guilty of "race crafting."[46] Like the spells recited by the witches and warlocks in Lovecraft Country, race has been conjured up from the depths; its divisiveness is devilish, necromanced into permanence.

Since its summoning, it's how we now define ourselves, see our world, and operate as a society. Though the concept of race has been debunked genealogically and theologically, it remains powerfully ingrained psychologically across the globe. We know its origin story, but we do not know its expiration date. Like a terminal disease, it seems resistant to all forms of treatment, simply mutating and adapting to its environment, even fooling the most susceptible that it no longer exists. As theologian Dr. Jarvas Williams stated, "race is a biological fiction but a sociological fact." The reality, though, is it has not always existed. In reality, the notion of race as a concept is relatively modern. Embracing deep humility and an insatiable curiosity again, I ask you, the reader, to pause and do some of your own pre-work to discover the origins of race. See the following questions below as you hunt the mythical supernatural entity called race.

Fig 6.1 Key Questions Concerning Race

Key Questions Concerning Race:

1. **When** was race created?
2. **Why** was race created?
3. **How** was race created?

What did you learn that surprised or frightened you?

Now there is a new bogeyman that has entered the building, a frightening suspect being accused of every unmentionable, unconscionable crime imaginable. Just mentioning the word race brings fear on the faces of adults and children alike. You may have heard of this big bad bogeyman. They or possibly It, it seems, has gone by a legion of names but is modernly known by the moniker CRT. You know of this evil I speak of. Or do you? Whenever someone asks, "Is this whole thing just CRT?" I push pause on the conversation and start asking curious questions. I ask questions to send the inquisitor on a quest to see if they are willing to lower the hatchet and possibly bury it. Here are the questions I ask, and credit to my brother Ken Shelton for the last one (which is my favorite):

Fig 6.2 Which CRT Are We Discussing?

If the response to these questions is, "I don't know the difference" or, "I don't know" or worse yet, "why don't you just tell me?" I simply reply, "you really should look them up for yourself, then we can talk afterward." Talking about race and racism can be daunting and even emotionally distressing for some individuals who have undergone traumatic experiences related to racism. To quote the homie, James Ford, I ask these questions to see if they are actually "good faith actors." Why would I engage in a conversation that feels more like a trap than an honest inquiry? Why would I willingly walk up that proverbial mountain and let you crucify me there? You can pick up your own cross and type into your smartphone faster than I can verbalize my thoughts and find out the distinction between one term and another and compare it to the literature on each topic that has existed for decades. Or you can listen to the sound bites of Tucker Carlson on Fox News, or Donald Trump bait and switch us into believing that even as White Nationalists invaded the U.S. Capitol on January 6th, "the real problem in America" is anti-patriotic propaganda such as CRT, teaching children to "hate their own country." As you do your research and find answers to questions that are pretty easy to find in the so-called information age, the only other thing I ask of you is to consider your sources.

An inordinate amount of time has been given to research and conversations clarifying that racism is not necessarily or solely an instance of individual prejudice. Let's set the record straight, especially for my white readers who may be offended by the sheer notion of being called privileged (i.e., personally benefiting from a social structure established for white supremacy). Just because you may not have negative feelings towards an individual because of their race does not mean that you do not participate in racist practices or perpetuate it by the policies you participate in or the privileges you enjoy because of its existence. Similar to what Ibrim X Kendi shares in *How to Be an Antiracist*, I too used to think that racist people created racist policies, and racist policies created by racist people helped create the cycle of structural racism.[47] Then I read our history and realized that racist thinking was created to justify systems of supremacy. That includes Black people perpetuating racist thoughts and white supremacy for selfish, individual gain. See the graphic below and let me do my best to explain:

Fig 6.3 The Hex of Racism

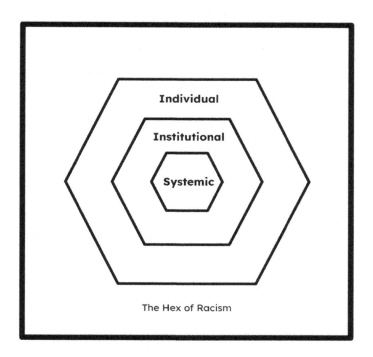

The Hex of Racism

On the top level is individual racism, that is, personal racist beliefs and actions that cause harm to a person of another race. When most think of racism, this is their only thought. Their view is that if they simply operate as "colorblind," the power of racism is thwarted. Little do they recognize that because we live in a race-based society, we all participate in its power structure, willingly or unwittingly. Because my own children are lighter-skinned, I am aware that they are afforded different privileges and given a pass more often than their darker-toned kin. It's maddening to me to consider how a home or car loan, a job interview, or a traffic violation may fare differently based on the fairness of one's complexion, a perplexing reality reinforced by a system of privilege often referred to as colorism. However, it is not enough to simply have a personal opposition to racist thoughts. One must see how racism is at play in all of society. Anything less is being satisfied with the status quo, which likely means remaining content with the personal advantages that you and others receive at the expense of others.

An interrogation of racism requires you to relinquish some privileges to which you have become accustomed. To not actively oppose racism is to allow it to continue. Therefore, we are all guilty of perpetuating racism due to inaction because racism is already in *action* by design. Because the machinery of systems will continue to run their course, the sorcery will continue its spellbinding unless the curse is broken on the institutional level- in every institution we ascribe to and participate in. Most relevant to the readers of this book, the specific forms of racism that exist in our schools must be delineated, dismantled, and destroyed. The curse of racism must be abolished at every level of our school environments. Can I get an Amen?

Where is Racism At Play In Your School?

As Ijeoma Oluo states in her acclaimed work, *So You Want to Talk About Race*, "If you live in this system of white supremacy, you are either fighting the system, or you are complicit."[48] The question, of course, is, what are the racist policies and procedures that are most prevalent in your educational setting that need to be delineated, dismantled, and destroyed? I hope that the curse of racism can be broken in schools because education is one of the most critical institutions in all of society. Schools assume the burden of cognitively, physically, and emotionally caring for tens of millions of children and young adults each year. Yet, whether you work at a racially segregated school or in a school that reflects intentional diversity and inclusion efforts, I am willing to bet racism is still at play in your setting. At *play*, let that sink in.

Think about the wordplay- evoking whimsical, effortless, and enjoyable. This is the curse of racism. It plays while we work to undo it. It plays us into thinking that it doesn't exist. It plays with our emotions and creates a rise in us at the mere mention of its presence. It plays people against one another like a child holds two action figures and uses one to punch the other. It plays while we pretend that the racial disparities in schools have little to do with us because we are all loving and caring and, in some cases, claim to be colorblind. Someone just read that line and said, "quit playing," either out of a feeling of remorse or rejection, or adulation that finally, someone else said it! Those aware of the ever-presence of racism are tired of playing games and refuse to look past it or ignore it whenever a discipline referral or reading scores are highlighted at the staff meeting. We want to say that our job is to help students find success, knowing that our Black and Brown students' young lives are often about a success that our schools have yet to define.

How do our students go beyond simply surviving to thriving? How do we correct our adults' attitudes, not just our kids, to believe that they have something our society needs beyond entertainment or institutional enslavement? These are questions, not answers. If I had the solution in my pocket, I would reveal it like a child shares a beautiful rock they found on the ground, its beauty containing nothing short of supernatural abilities. If I had such a magical remedy, I would not be so cruel as to hide it from you. The truth is the insidious demonic force that we call racism must be first called out for what it is and not called a farce. It must be delineated, dismantled, then destroyed. My next question is, if you could go beyond your imagination and not close your eyes but open them to the terrifying reality of spiritual warfare at play in just the institution of education alone, what would you see?

Fig 6.4 Examples of Racism

Tokenism[49]

Tokenism is the symbolic inclusion of numerical minorities within a group, usually for the sake of appearances rather than for inclusiveness or true diversity.

Racial Profiling[50]

Racial profiling is defined as the use of race or ethnicity, or proxies thereof, by law enforcement officials as a basis for judgments of criminal suspicion.

Implicit Bias[51]

Implicit Biases are negative associations expressed automatically that people unknowingly hold and that that affect our understanding, actions and decisions; also known as unconscious or hidden bias.

Centering[52]

Centering or white centering is the centering of white people, white values, white norms and white feelings over everything and everyone else.

Stereotype Threat[53]

Stereotype Threat is the threat of being viewed through the lens of a negative stereotype or the fear of doing something that would inadvertently confirm that stereotype.

Microaggression[54]

Microaggression is the verbal, nonverbal and environmental slights, snubs, insults or actions, whether intentional or unintentional, which communicate hostile, derogatory or negative messages to target persons based solely upon discriminatory belief systems.

So here we are again, confronting some of the most horrifying issues that we wish we could simply banish by closing our eyes. If you've ever seen the movie *The Sixth Sense*, you know what I am referring to when I say that our schools are haunted. Issues such as Implicit Bias, Tokenism, Profiling, Centering, Stereotype Threat, and Microaggressions are ever-present and have been hanging around long before we finally gain the awareness to notice them. Next question, when you consider the terms and their definitions, does a particular instance readily come to mind? Was it an offense that you witnessed, or were you the offender? Even as a Black male educator committed to dismantling and destroying racism in my midst, I have failed frequently at standing up against the assault of microaggressions and tokenism directed at me or towards others in my presence.

I often do mental calculus, considering whether or not it is worth calling shenanigans based on my position or relationship to others in the situation. It is an unfortunate reality that I often first consider the question, "what do I have to lose?" before advocating for myself or others. It seems that I am prone to not be as bold as I would like to be until someone does something so egregious that the piling on of offenses amounts to me going full beast mode and telling people what they need to hear without caution or filter.

Like the time I was co-leading training for a group of educators, and the superintendent decided to take the stage to share the organization's commitment to anti-racism. Then in an attempt to speak to the visible lack of diversity on their leadership team, he did the unthinkable. He pointed to the one person of color on their staff in the room and said something to the effect of "it definitely took too long for us to promote our first Black person to leadership...." I about died inside! We were just getting started, and the person in charge that hired us to help them in their anti-racism training just committed like four offenses, all in one short two-minute speech. I would like to say that I immediately called the gentleman out (payment be damned!). Except I didn't. I froze. I did the mental calculus thing and looked at the person he was speaking about to see if I could recognize pain in his gaze, but instead, I saw a wry smile and a physical and verbal waiving off of the metaphorical spotlight shining on him. I reasoned that if he was ok, I could be ok, and we could deal with this incident later as part of our debrief. The reality is that I did not consider how the offense affected the individual and how it affected the room. As Dr. Martin Luther King Jr. said, "Whatever affects one directly, affects all indirectly. I can never be what I ought to be until you are what you ought to be. This is the interrelated structure of reality."[55] At that moment, I did not choose to be brave. I allowed racism to perpetuate. I got played by my own fears. Racism won again.

How Might You Solve Racism in Schools?

It is impossible to list an exhaustive list of how racism manifests in schools and how I have personally navigated them. That said, if there is one form of racism that comes to mind just because of its sheer repetitiveness, it's microaggressions. Just mentioning microaggressions makes some cringe, either because it is something that they know they have witnessed multiple times or because they take issue with the word itself. Slights, biting comments, backhanded compliments, etc., don't feel micro at all. They amount to a consistent barrage of abuse that some deny or simply dismiss with an "oops" when someone says, "ouch." It's not micro when cutting comments just keep coming, and old wounds are reopened. Some are never allowed to heal. Though not lynching, it's Lingchi, death by a thousand cuts.

Like Mystery Mix Now-and-Laters, microaggressions may be hard to identify from the outside, but anyone who has tasted it knows its distinct flavor profile. Unlike traditional overt racism (e.g., cross burnings and Rosa Parks's bus boycott days), racial microaggressions can be very subtle, ambiguous, and fuzzy in nature and therefore harder to label.[54] Microaggressions taste like blood pooling from the inside of your cheeks after being open hand slapped across the face. Maybe due to melanin, the victim's face doesn't show the handprint of the offender, but the offended still let out a wail, and if you run your hand across the struck area, you can feel the welt. This is all metaphorically speaking, but the reality is that others will minimize the offense because it is not obvious to them. That is what we call microaggressions. They resemble gaslighting or dog-whistling, or a number of other verbal offenses that the offender can counter with, "that's not what I said" or "that's not what I meant" or even worse, "you're just hearing what you want to hear." It's plausible deniability when perpetrated by the intentional bigot. It's privilege on display when the ignorant get a pass for simply not knowing better. It also places the burden on the victim and negates any accountability on the perpetrator.

One example out of an uncountable number of infractions I recently recalled on Twitter (see #BlackIntheIvory) was when I applied for entry into my master's program and had to deal with what some would call a microaggression from the department chair. I had spent weeks putting together my early entry application only to watch her hurriedly thumb through the pages, skipping past my essay, my letters of recommendation, and finally stopping on my grades. Finally, she broke her silence with the words, "you got a B in Qualitative Analysis?" Then she looked up and said, "Well, you are Black… ok, you're in."

According to Columbia University psychologist Derald Wing Sue, what I experienced at that moment is also known as a microinsult.[56] This department chairperson was guilty of saying that I didn't measure up, yet I was expected to underperform in a high-level math class. Imagine my countenance at that moment. Despite the offense, if I wanted to ensure I was accepted into the program, what could I do besides put on a fake smile and express gratitude? To strike back would be a monumental mistake. She was the gatekeeper of my future, and I had to decide to protect myself beyond the moment. So, whether I agree with the terminology of microaggression or not, I understand the reality of the existence of this thing we call microaggressions. I know it because this was an instance, like many others, that I felt the sting, and yet when I shared it with many white friends, many dismissed it or attempted to explain what she may have "really" meant. This action, by many of my friends, is also known as microinvalidation. "Micro" only because it was hard for others to see, but I felt it. And it still hurts. As the Marvel character, Hope Van Dyne explained in the movie Antman and the Wasp, "When you're small, energy's compressed, so you have the force of a 200-pound man behind a fist a 100th of an inch wide. You're like a bullet. You punch too hard, you kill someone." Microaggressions not only sting, but they can also be deadly over time.

I have moved away from using the language "walking a mile in another person's shoes." It's limited in scope and insufficient to do the job of empathy. To literally walk a mile in someone else's shoes would mean that the person would have to have the same shoe size, would only walk a mile, and then would remove the shoes to return to the comfort of the kicks they usually wear. In the instance above, I used an example of something that happened to me. I performed research to try and make sense of the situation, but if you are not a person of color and never had to endure a daily dose of belittling comments and side-eyes because race is what people want to point at as the reason for some strange phenomenon they don't quite understand, then, please do not insert yourself into the narrative. That's another form of racism called *Centering*. It's not about you. Empathy requires listening and caring for someone else that has experienced pain. It acknowledges your inability to even imagine the amount of pain another is feeling. It simply requires listening, being close, and as the Bible prescribes in Romans 12:15, "...weep with those that weep, mourn with those that mourn."

How might this issue be solved in a new way? I mean, an entirely new way? Hat tip to my colleague and play-cousin Rohiatou Siby for familiarizing me with the "Ouch/Oops" protocol. Here is how it works: If a person says something offensive, the target or a bystander can say, "ouch," to signal to the group that the words used or action made were hurtful. Here's the thing- anyone can say it, not just the person the action or comment was addressed to. This is key because bystanders can be affected as well. In some cases, the bystander can be more offended, simply due to the fact that the offended is unfortunately used to being marginalized, used to being told, "don't take things so seriously," used to doing the mental calculus and considering the cost of saying something in a particular setting based on a certain offense. Therefore, the bystander, the ally, needs to be equipped and empowered to take up the fight, so the victim of vitriol isn't gagged by the constant gaslighting of an individual that is (intentionally or unintentionally) abusing them. It is an exhausting exercise to defend oneself constantly, explain the offense, educate the offender, and consider the potential consequences of challenging a superior. Every school needs to set up cultural dynamics where all are invited to challenge racism when they sniff it, and the burden needs to be on the community, not the individual, to address it.

Take another example of a microaggression that is often overlooked but used to harm students from the onset. I heard a teacher educate her class on the concept of "learning styles" with the intention of empowering them to advocate for themselves. I listened in horror, even as I picked up my laptop to fire off an email to the teacher with article links to help them understand the fundamental flaws in the lesson that she was delivering. I offered an article to read and an invitation to research the topic more. Propagating myths that have been disproven multiple times over is a microaggression that harms students. Did you know that the concept of "learning styles" is not only a myth, but is deeply rooted in racism? I hope you are opening a search engine now to fact-check me!

Community commitments can be powerful verbal and visceral responses to the race-crafting that horrifies people and haunts our hallways. To break the spell means to not only speak truth into the power of institutions and authority figures but the spiritual realm that mystically hovers over it all. Might I suggest your community create a creed to be declared as a form of community commitment?

"We" statements, such as the following excerpt from a community creed created by Dr. Lucretia Berry, can serve a community well. Imagine your school faculty all gathering in a faculty meeting room and declaring:

> *We consider our contribution to the healing process, and*
> *we ask ourselves, "Are my thoughts and actions helpful,*

hopeful, inspiring, and encouraging? Am I contributing to healing and change?" We do our homework. We do our research. We recognize race ideology as the GIANT ENEMY and people as victims of its deception, Legacy, and intimidation! WE WILL NOT SLING ROCKS AT PEOPLE! WE WILL BE CREATORS of safe spaces.[57]

Obviously, even if microaggressions were obliterated from the institution of education entirely, that would not come close to eradicating all of racism. However, this approach is a start, an opportunity to build a culture of accountability versus compliance. A culture where even those in authority are accountable to the community to elevate equity of voice. Within that culture, policies can be examined, practices evaluated, and holistic anti-racism work implemented. Want to eradicate the terror of racism in your midst? My suggestion is to start with calling your entire community into the healing work of eliminating the terrorizing tactic of microaggressions. You may find my personal thoughts limited or short-sighted, which is why I invite you to call in the most marginalized in your midst, call out the problems of racism in your setting, and set goals to eradicate them, lest they haunt us forever.

If you could eradicate one form of racism in schools, what would you do? How would you share your solution?

C H A P T E R   7

Fighting for Civil Rights

The greatest movement for social justice our country has ever known is the civil rights movement and it was totally rooted in a love ethic.
– bell hooks

Where Have Our Activists Gone?

On July 17, 2020, a dark cloud hovered over the world. It wasn't a new report on the devastating effects of COVID-19 (though that was happening). It wasn't a report of something nonsensical or divisive being Tweeted by the 45th President of the United States (though that was also absolutely happening). That was the morning that I saw trending #RIPJohnLewis. Hours later, we also learned of the loss of Rev C.T. Vivian, another friend and contemporary of Dr. Martin Luther King Jr. Just earlier in the year, we lost Elijah Cummings. One by one, devastating blow after devastating blow, we lost several stalwarts of the Civil Rights era from the 1960s, leaving us to deal with the madness of 2020 seemingly on our own. Amid a new Civil Rights era, we would not be competing with the actual voices of the old heads clamoring for "civil disobedience" vs. "by any means necessary." Instead, we would have to listen to our ancestors and the lessons they taught us, knowing they were with us in spirit, though no longer in body. They embodied the commitment and courage necessary for all of us. Whether we played the role of onlookers or "onward soldiers," there was a new civil rights movement underway that the world was bearing witness to. The summer of 2020 was hot. Many cities were ablaze with protests and demands for justice to be made for the tragic murders of several Black men and women by militarized police officers and militiamen. We in the Black community were losing our heroes, losing our loved ones, and losing our minds.

John Lewis was 80 years old when he died of pancreatic cancer in Atlanta, Georgia. During his life would serve 17 terms in the U.S. House of Representatives fighting for the same civil rights he dedicated himself to as a young man. I imagine Lewis became what a teacher told him he could or could not become. Either way, he would become a force to be reckoned with, whether or not he was recommended to be student body president, I still remember the day he hugged the first Black President. In many ways, Barack Obama became, because of what John Lewis had already become. At the age of 21, he was one of the original Freedom Riders brutally assaulted in Rock Hill, South Carolina, for trying to enter a whites-only waiting room in 1961. He was 25 when he had his head cracked open by the baton of state troopers while crossing the Edmund Pettus Bridge in Selma, Alabama, on what would be called "Bloody Sunday" on March 7, 1965. That fateful day would be one of the significant catalysts leading to President Lyndon B. Johnson signing the Voting Rights Act four months later. The thing that gets me is how young he was! Little did we know that he was just getting started. I'm grateful that he lived as long as he did to inspire many to take up the banner of "Good Trouble."

Ahmaud Arbery was 26 years old when he was murdered near Brunswick in Glynn County, Georgia, on February 23, 2020. He was suspected of stealing from a construction site and was hunted, attacked, and shot in the middle of the day by a neighborhood resident and his son. His death reminds many of us of Treyvon Martin, of Emmet Till, of the countless but not nameless young men that have been lynched by a white mob for crossing a white line. The tweets and Facebook comments from the uneducated and educators alike said things to the effect of, "if he had just…" which is code for, stay in his place, not look suspicious, not run from those encircling him, taunting him, hopping out of a truck with a shotgun in hand to supposedly apprehend, this young Black man. This "citizen's arrest," this unhooded neighborhood watch, this tiny clan of runaway slave police murdered this young man for running through the neighborhood in which he lived, for running from men pursuing him by truck… and for fighting back. Many watched his execution replayed repeatedly on social media. My wife saw it online before I could click on it. Ironically, I had just come in the door from a jog in our neighborhood. She looked up at me with tears in her eyes and said, "Please don't watch the video. It will undo you." It still does. To this day, I have not watched the video in its entirety. I read the reports, I saw the footage on the news up until the point where they blocked Ahmaud's path, and one of the assailants jumped out of the truck. I stopped there, I turned away. I know what came next, and I don't need to see the rest to be further traumatized by it.

Breonna Taylor was 26 years old when she was gunned down in her own home by plainclothes police in Louisville, Kentucky, on March 13, 2020. She was an ER technician and aspiring nurse whose biggest mistake was formerly dating a known drug dealer. As a result, her residence was the target of a strategic raid. Though her former boyfriend was already apprehended at his own home some 10 miles away, her door was busted open, and her current boyfriend, Kenneth Walker, shot in what he called self-defense to an intrusion. A hail spray of bullets littered the apartment. Breonna was shot six times by Metro police. They said they properly identified themselves. They said they were returning fire after being fired upon. They also said they were doing a drug bust without sound evidence of any drugs or trafficking activity from the apartment. There's no bodycam footage for us to dissect or reject. Just the forensics of a bullet-riddled scene and the testimony of the police and Walker. As I walked alone through my neighborhood one night, I listened to a news story detailing the then-known facts. I slowed my steps and eventually stopped and wept. I listened to the 911 call from Walker, who sobbed in terror, "I don't know what happened … somebody kicked in the door and shot my girlfriend." Breonna received no medical attention the night she was killed. She was not rushed to a hospital. Her body lay in the hallway of the apartment for hours.

George Floyd was 46 years old when he was murdered by police in Minneapolis, Minnesota, on May 25, 2020. He was arrested for suspicion of using a counterfeit bill. One officer, Derek Chauvin, put his knee on the back of Floyd's neck, and the entire weight of his body pressed down on an already handcuffed man for 9 minutes and 29 seconds. I've thought about that sheer amount of time so often. Are you a runner or jogger? Consider the distance you could run in 9 min and 29 seconds. Is it a mile? Slightly more or slightly less? Whether on a track or a trail, consider all of what you would encounter, the people you would see, the terrain you would navigate, the trees, or the traffic lights during that nearly 10-minute run. When complete, you would take slow, deliberate breaths in your nose and out your mouth, giving your respiratory system much-needed recovery. As you check your heart rate and feel the slight burn in your lungs and the fatigue in your legs, imagine, in that same amount of time, a man pressed his knee on another man's neck, asphyxiating him through his cries for help, his cries for, "Momma" and his resigned statement, "You're gonna kill me." Two other officers helped restrain a handcuffed man and face down on the pavement with a knee to his neck. Another police officer kept guard so none from the gathered crowd could intervene. As Floyd labored to hold onto life, his death was recorded for all of us to witness his last exhale.

Floyd's agonizing exclamation of "I can't breathe" was eerily reminiscent of Eric Garner, an 18-year-old unarmed black man killed in 2014 after being put in a chokehold by New York City Police. His murder reminded us of Michael Brown, an 18-year-old unarmed Black man shot six times by the police in Ferguson, Missouri, killed in 2014. His murder reminded us of Sandra Bland, a 26-year-old Black woman who was found hanged in a Waller County jail cell in 2015. Her death reminded us of Philando Castile, a 32-year-old Black man shot in front of his girlfriend and child in 2016. His death reminded us of Atatiana Jefferson, who was shot to death in her home while playing video games with her eight-year-old nephew by a police officer who was supposed to be answering a "welfare call" because her door was open at 2:30 a.m. in Fort Worth, Texas. Her death reminded us of so many murders that went unrecorded, that were determined as justified homicides, whether there was a gun, weed, or a past criminal record. Police and private citizens seem to be able to kill Black and Brown people with impunity, and it all harkens back to the trauma that runs generationally through our veins. Fear chases us like dogs, chastens us like watchmen, and lynches us publicly. Our murders are retold from memories, recorded on paper, and watched on cell phones.

These are just some of the names that have marked the movement, the chants for justice, the emblems emblazoned on city streets and sports arenas: Black Lives Matter! They matter enough for the world to take notice. They matter enough to interrupt your regular routine, your nightly news, your conversations at work, your church sermon, your classroom lesson, your existence... cause their existence mattered! I write these words with tears. I type angrily and violently, with no regard for these keys. If they break, they break. The cost of this keyboard will never come close to the lives of so many people that have been broken, not only by the police officers that murdered them, not only by the grand juries that refused to prosecute them but the public that bemoans the phrase, "Black Lives Matter" because they find it offensive. Because they choose to ignore the evidence of the injustice committed by our civil servants and the explanation of the terminology of Black Lives Matter. They counter it with "All Lives Matter" or "Blue Lives Matter." I will not waste my breath anymore or even my words on this page to re-explain once again something so basic that common sense should have kicked in by now and moved you beyond the slogan and moved you past the bumper sticker and the lawn sign, and the performative post on social media saying that you believe or you support, or you love. Our society is fighting over semantics more than the sanctity of life, and I am tired of playing the debate game.

I can only think, what would Martin say about what has happened within the last decade? Though beloved today, I am reminded mainly because his words have been carefully extracted from speeches and sound bites, reduced to tiny particles no longer bearing the weight of the paragraphs of lectures and sermons he gave. I challenge you to go and read his Letter from Birmingham Jail or listen to his final interview given to NBC in 1967. Set a timer for 9 minutes and 29 seconds and listen to his words, both relevant for then as well as today.

Listen to his prophetic words and see if you can hear the echoes of the chant, "Black Lives Matter!" or at least they should. Whatever you do, please do not let some of the recent convictions of the perpetrators of these crimes or the civil suit settlements fool you into thinking that the problem is finally solved or that justice has finally come. If that is your mindset, then ask those around you, again, the voices of those most proximate to the pain of institutional injustice.

Keith Lamont Scott was 43 years old when he was shot and killed by police officers in Charlotte, North Carolina, in 2016. I live in Charlotte, and at the time, I worked at a charter school located in the heart of the city, Uptown, as we call it. When the police bodycam of the shooting was set to be released, the mayor warned many of the businesses and schools that there would likely be social unrest, so we closed school for a couple of days. Those evenings were marked by confrontations between police and protestors, tear gas, broken windows, and a lot of media attention. The shooting not only happened in my city of residence, but right around the corner from my home of ten years, right across the street from the college campus I attended, and in the same apartment complex I hung out with friends who lived there when I used to work on campus. It was literally too close to home. When the footage was released and the video was spotty, and though the police yelled, "drop the gun," I also heard on the tape his girlfriend yells out, "Don't shoot him, he has no weapon!" So, when a photo was later released of a gun beside the body, considering the history of police corruption and countless stories of murder cover-ups and false arrests involving people that look like me, please understand my skepticism. When we returned to school, the administration sent out emails to the staff giving tips on having conversations with the students. I still remember the first class where the entire 4th grade was gathered, and one of the teachers asked a question or two to the kids, and then he looked over their heads and saw my eyes from across the room. He asked, "Hey, Mr. Lanier, are you ok?" I spun around in shame, attempting to catch my tears, but my lungs and tear ducts all caught me by surprise and betrayed me at the moment. I charged out of the room sobbing. In all of the communication to address the emotional needs of 10 and 11-year-olds, there was no effort to address the pain of the 40-year-old Black male in the building. Keith Lamont Scott could have been me.

Why Should Your Students Care?

The death of John Lewis conjured all of this up for me. The year 2020 and the ensuing white mob resistance to liberty and justice for all in 2021 conjured all of this up for me. The existence of ICE raids that separate children from their parents, that shackle those looking for freedom and cage them like cattle, the elimination of DACA by the administration of the 45th president, the signing of Executive Order 13769, also known as the "Muslim ban", the racism of this country being redubbed as terrorism, and the terrorism of this country being redubbed as patriotism. These are the times that we have been living in. To combat these terrors, to solve these problems, and to overcome the actions of agencies that affect our very existence requires a commitment to real-world problem-solving. We don't have time for the trivial. We don't have time for solving puzzles, memorizing irrelevant material, or cramming to regurgitate propaganda guised as history or literature. We must unite our students and activate their commitment to our so-called democratic ideals, values, and principles. It is time that we discard all of the things that don't matter, so we can actually solve the problems that truly matter. The loss of John Lewis was emblematic in many ways. This is a new era, but it reminds us of our past. Who will lead us moving forward while enduring the trauma in the necessary work of #GoodTrouble?

Dear teachers, connect your content to not only the topics that are of interest to your students but specifically, to the civil rights concerns that affect them on the institutional level and plague the communities they truly care about. On the next page is a list of just a few examples to spark great dialogue within your educational community:

Fig 7.1 Examples of Civil Rights

Voter Suppression[58]

Voter Suppression is a political strategy — usually at the party-level but sometimes conducted by zealous individuals — designed to prevent a group of would-be voters from registering to vote or voting.

Censorship[59]

Censorship the suppression of words, images, or ideas that are "offensive," happens whenever some people succeed in imposing their personal political or moral values on others.

Housing Inequality[60]

Housing Inequality is a form of economic inequality related to widespread disparities in quality/availability of homes.

Criminal Justice[61]

Criminal Justice is a generic term that refers to the laws, procedures, institutions, and policies at play before, during, and after the commission of a crime.

Police Brutality[62]

Police Brutality is a civil rights violation that occurs when a police officer acts with excessive force by using an amount of force with regards to a civilian that is more than necessary.

Educational Inequality[63]

Educational Inequality is the disproportionate distribution of academic resources, such as school funding, qualified teachers and staff and adequate school supplies to socially excluded communities.

Which civil rights topic grieves you the most and why?

If you are a math teacher reading these words, I hope they motivate you to be one who positively molds the next great mind and heart of the civil rights leader that can spark a movement of change to combat the deranged that truly believe that their *manifest destiny* is to subtract and divide with a cascade of lies- instead of adding and multiplying the pieces of pie that this so-called great country cannot hide from those that are hungry. As Bettina Love states, "Too often we think the work of fighting oppression is just intellectual. The real work is personal, emotional, spiritual, and communal."[64] Civic engagement and fighting for civil rights is a practice for the masses, not just the activists. Move beyond simply solving equations and inequalities to introducing inequities and the many variables that create them. Have your students literally do the math, count the cost, and calculate the reward of every institution prioritizing restitution for the most marginalized in their industry.

How Can You Get Them Involved?

If you are a language literacy teacher, my encouragement is to have your students use their text to identify injustice in its various forms. Or what Paulo Freire has termed, *conscientization*, or conscientização. It's a Portuguese term that is loosely interpreted as "critical consciousness," or the ability to intervene in reality to change it.[65] Language teachers do not merely teach the language and its translations into English, but rather how the English and the Spanish both colonized entire countries and established the powerful institutions that denied the indigenous people the equality of treatment, access, and justice deserving of all peoples. If you teach Black and Brown students, their connection to your text depends on their felt opportunity to correct the injustices they see and sense all around them. We often boast in education about integrating the so-called "4Cs" for 21st Century Learning (communication, collaboration, critical thinking, and creativity). Still, we rarely introduce a 5th C that makes all those others possible- Connection. Not just connection to the teacher, though that is without a doubt a necessity, connection to the content itself. If your only answer to the question of, "Why should they care?" is simply "because it is on the test" or "they need to know this for success," then I challenge you to dig deeper and dialogue with your pupils to discover what they really care about.

If you are a Health Science teacher, please do your students some justice to speak to the injustice they will have to endure in their lifetimes. Speak to their need to monitor their heart rates, their breathing cadence, the tingling sensations that emerge in their bodies as they emotionally endure the trauma of gaslit comments and toxic policies that separate and subjugate families, historically and currently. Science teachers, connect your content on habitations and ecosystems to the proximate problems of food deserts, air quality alerts, and hurricanes that devastate not only because of global warming but poorly funded levies in marginalized communities. Remind them that they must mind what they intake, not only physically but emotionally, to preserve their lives and to have enough energy to fight for civil rights.

History and social studies teachers here's an idea, set the stage for engaging the topic of civil rights by having your students read and do pre-work researching the 1st Amendment to the US. Constitution. Even the typical "What did you notice, what do you wonder" exercise may reveal much about what your students already understand and how their previous thoughts are challenged simply by going to the original text and not just the pontifications of pundits and propagators. The 1st Amendment reads:

> *Congress shall make no law respecting an establishment of religion, or prohibiting the free exercise thereof; or abridging the freedom of speech, or of the press; or the right of the people peaceably to assemble, and to petition the Government for a redress of grievances.*

Your students may notice that the scope of the 1st Amendment is limited to the Federal Government but does not limit State legislatures (though it later did after the ratification of the 14th Amendment) or private institutions, such as social media platforms, workplaces, and schools. Therefore the 1st Amendment doesn't mean your job can't fine or fire you, nor does it mean that the culture can't cancel you or that you cannot be held accountable for your opinion or actions. Another student may notice the language concerning respecting an establishment of religion... Again, more discussion is to be had about clarifying what this means and what it does not mean for schools and individual citizens. The goal of the demarginalizing designer is not to push one's own agenda or the topics they would like to protest, but to help make clear what the students don't understand, giving the students or staff the resources needed and teaching them the skills to explore further, and to discover what they are most passionate about and why.

You may have noticed that I have made little attempt throughout this book to connect how admin can use this exercise to connect to the teachers' passions. Suppose you are thinking about how this focus on civil rights can be used as part of your professional development. In that case, that is completely fine, and I welcome you to make that translation upward, but how often do we think that students are to follow our lead instead of the other way around? I once worked at a particular school that made many attempts to connect to the community through service learning and pushed their 8th graders into learning about governmental laws and how to lobby for Bills to be passed on certain topics. The one problem that I had that I spoke strongly against at the forefront was that they organized the students into action groups based on the passions of the adult teachers and administrators that served as advisors instead of originating from the students themselves. Thankfully the critique was heard, and the program was adjusted. Still, my point is our pursuit should always be to follow our students' lead and work alongside them, offering them wisdom and teaching them the skills necessary to solve the problems they are most passionate about. Quoting Paolo Freire again, "The teacher is no longer merely the one-who-teaches, but one who is himself taught in dialogue with the students, who in turn while being taught also teach. They become jointly responsible for a process in which all grow."[67] If any of us call ourselves educators, whether classroom teachers, paraprofessionals, building or district-level administrators or service providers, we are all employed because of the existence of students. Let's do the work of dialoguing with them to discover what matters most to them, the ways in which they have been marginalized, and engage in the deep work of co-designing their future.

Asking a question outside of the norm will often reveal what our textbooks have ignored. Often our research on laws and statutes lacks curiosity, in my opinion. Our push as educators is to help our students not merely memorize names and dates associated with different topics of interest but to recognize the locations and their relative distance, so the students can begin to relate. Here's just an example, but consider the question,

"Where did police brutality begin?". With a bit of research, the students may uncover the heinousness of police beatings and murder of civilians was not limited to the rural South, often regarded as an abstract land of horror for many youths that only know the urban context in which they reside.

Intrigue may lead them to do an online search for "Police Brutality Beginning" which revealed an article that points to instances of police violence in major metropolitans such as Boston, Chicago, Detroit, Los Angeles, New York, and Philadelphia.[66] In looking for the location in which these atrocities began, dates begin to band together political corruption and policing dating back to at least the 17th century. Locating the exact location of the beginning of brutality by location seems inscrutable, nonetheless, research revealed that the term "police brutality" was seemingly first used by the American press in 1872, when the Chicago Tribune reported on the beating of a civilian under arrest at the Harrison Street Police Station.[68] Of course it should be noted that this is simply the first use of the term, not its origin by definition, nonetheless, students can discover that police brutality is a longstanding problem, specifically in the cities in which many of our Black and Brown students reside.

For the teacher, asking why the problem matters to you may hit its limit based on your proximity to the pain of any of the social issues listed above. Nevertheless, you may have compassion and empathy already deep into your bones based on your own observations and experience of injustice. If you drive a car to work and do not worry about police tailgating you for several blocks, obviously running your plates, and anticipating that you make a mistake (like not hitting your blinker or coming to a complete stop at a stop sign) as you were distracted by the police car in your rearview and you panic with raised heart rate.

If you have not watched the TV and thought that a person who was harassed then hauled into a car, never to be seen alive again, looks like you (and the ones that die instead of de-escalated often do), then my request is to simply observe the pain all around you. Allow the sobs of your students to become audible to you, allow their salty stream-like tears to wash over you, and their eyes to stare deeply into yours, either as a form of connection or correction (you know the look that says, I don't think you truly understand). Here's a science lesson for you, there's this thing called intergenerational epigenetic inheritance, which is the concept that trauma can be traced even in our DNA. Therefore, when a student or staff member sees the replay of the killing of an unarmed Black teen, what is triggered is not only a connection based on appearances, but the soul cries of their ancestors.

Hear how they already care deeply about some of the topics because they infringe on their current civil liberties and how they don't need a textbook to tell them that parts of society are obviously corrupt and that the powers that be seem to be profiting from the profiling, and criminalization which leads to mass-incarceration, which also leads to their disenfranchisement. They may not have all the definitions down or the right words to fully codify all they have witnessed into cogent sentences, but if you choose to listen, you can later help them with their naming conventions. All around them, they have witnessed the discrimination laws de facto or de jure, based on race, religion, gender, age, or disability that need to be discovered, distinguished, dismantled, and destroyed. Whatever makes them angry enough to fight, whatever burdens them so much they feel like giving up, there is your opportunity to connect your content to civic engagement, from humanities to human rights, from science to social good, from mathematics to dismantling the mechanics of injustice in their school and their society. Even if you do not know exactly how, make this your commitment, and bring your own life experience, training, connections to people or organizations, and understanding of systems to the direct dialogue with your students as you wrestle with how to integrate your content.

When I was preparing to become the Director for Passion Projects during my teaching career, I found myself calling upon every resource I could to develop this program. Sure, there were things online, books to read, podcasts to hear, but the best for me was calling up friends of established programs and listening to how they got started and what factors I should consider. Here was my commitment- I wanted to create a systematic approach to real-world problem-solving that connected to the passions of my students. Unlike many of the other programs I had read about, I was not interested in simply having my students explore and share their appreciation for music, for instance. Instead, I wanted to tap into their love for the community and the problems they witnessed that caused them emotional turmoil. I wanted to know how a student's love for music might connect to their concern for those experiencing homelessness. What might they design if their creativity connected to their concerns?

Now consider, what might it look like if a student paired their interest in video games with their passion for eliminating police brutality? What if that same student (along with others) came up with the concept of a "call out the bad cop" training simulator styled after the popular multiplayer game, Among Us? Or what if they come up with the concept of cop cams being automatically activated when a service weapon is removed from the officer's holster? Or if the student with a passion for virtual reality imagines that the cameras are designed with concave lenses so police footage can include a wider perspective that can be viewed if a case is investigated? With so much talk about "defunding the police," some may think of ways to demilitarize the police force, to reimagine them as protectors that are accountable to the public in which they serve. I am not pretending to have the solution to the many civil rights issues above or even the example utilized here. Still, if we allow our students to engage with the problems that enrage them, personal passion becomes an opportunity to connect pedagogy with community upliftment.

These issues are not only personal to me, but to those I care about. Because I am no longer full-time in the classroom, I rely primarily on conversations with teachers and special visits to classrooms to hear students' perspectives directly. As a father of four children who at the time of the writing of this book were stratified across elementary, middle, and high school, I am blessed to get their perspectives regularly. So, I leave you with this poem written by my oldest daughter:

Fig 7.2 "Fight"

"Fight," by Karis Lanier

CONCLUSION

Putting All Cards on The Table

We must use time creatively, in the knowledge
that the time is always ripe to do right.
– MLK

What Other Questions Do You Have?

I've written this entire book with the hopes of moving you. To see one person's perspective, combined with the perspectives I have witnessed, and hopefully given you enough space to interject your thoughts in the margins. But it's time now to move your ideas beyond the margins and into action. It's time.

As stated early in this book, this work was aimed at your heart and mind, and inevitably, there are those of you who now need something to do with your feet and your hands. Hopefully, the right buttons have been pushed to provoke you to dive right in and battle against every bias, defeat every form of discrimination, eradicate racism, and fight for civil rights within your school communities and beyond.

Allow me to let you in on what is probably the worst kept secret at this point- this book is an elaboration on the equity expansion of a design thinking process I collaboratively created with dozens of students and educators called, Solve in Time!® For those of you unfamiliar and legitimately had no idea, welcome!

141

For those of you who knew all along and read through the pages just wanting me to call it out, I'll inform you as to why I chose to remain cryptic versus overt.

Reason number one, this book was intended to make you consider that the people in the margins matter most in solving real and relevant problems, not the process you utilize for solving said problems. I have chosen to emphasize the tool I created until now because I want to remind all design thinkers that the tool you use is tertiary. Remember this- *people* over process.

Reason number two, I wanted to center this book on many of the most real and relevant issues to the Black and Brown students and staff that comprise your educational community- without compromise and without apology. I began writing this book at the beginning of a global pandemic when the issues mentioned in part two were simply highlighted, not heightened. For those that began reading journals and books and listening to podcasts that focused on social injustice and inequities of various forms, your eyes were simply opened to every day, the long-standing reality of our existence.

Reason number three, I have held back the explicit calling out of Solve in Time!® as a design thinking process because I wanted you to see it applied, not simply explained. In my community, people are accustomed to being given rules, guidelines, and recommended paths to success in nearly every social setting, except when it comes to matters that are solely within their own control. This book was written out of freedom, not bondage. This book was written with the literary liberation that Langston penned his poems, and Lauren unleashed her lyricism. Prose and poetry, run-on sentences, full expression without fear of not giving the publishing company what they want, or not meeting the superficial bar that is somehow lower, yet called higher than the standard my people hold themselves to. Like Mahaila calling from the crowd, "Tell them about the dream, Martin." I put down my script and simply shared from my heart and allowed my lips to breathe out, as I regularly wept while recounting painful realities that have been real and relevant to me, to my family, to my community, for as long as I am aware that we have existed in spaces that are not distinctly our own.

So, time to answer some of the questions you may have been asking:

Yes, this book is an unpacking of the four expansion packs that accompany the Equity add-on of Solve in Time!®

Yes, I have hoped that educators who are familiar with Solve in Time!® would be hit with their own M. Night Shyamalan moment when they got to this section of the book.

Yes, I hope that someone just seconds ago wrote, "I knew it!" in the margins of this book.

Yes, I have intentionally asked *Who, What, When, Where, Why,* and *How* questions throughout each chapter in this book to model the inquiry-based nature of Solve in Time!®. However, if you look back, you may notice that I have also followed the process of identifying the problem, doing research, seeking to understand, asking how I might solve this problem, and sharing my ideas in written form.

Yes, I am aware that I am still not fully explaining exactly what Solve in Time!® is, and that is by design. Nevertheless, I hope I have made you curious enough to look beyond the words in this book and do your own research on things you do not quite understand.

Yes, I have highlighted only a few of the many issues included in the Equity add-on pack because they represent the issues that have pained me the most in my limited years. Thank you for getting more proximate to my pain.

Yes, you can read this book from cover to cover, read it in reverse order, and realize it is designed as intentionally cyclical, not linear. It is still a design thinking book, remember.

Yes, I am aware that some of the chapters are dense and require lots of unpacking and research, and dialogue with others. I hope you have done this in your community and listened to the voices of those that are typically listened to the least. I hope that you will continue.

Yes, I am also aware of the contradictory nature of such a work like this. I emphasize the need to listen to others but mostly share my own perspective based on my own limited experience and education.

Yes, I am also aware of the inherent contradiction of advocating for multiple forms of expression while mostly only offering you written word. Still, this book consists mostly of written words- not vocal recordings, cinematic or graphical visual display. Like most academia, this book is limited to a singular medium of expression. Like the author, this book is very limited, but it will hopefully do much more than expected.

Yes, I have even more to offer you. And so do the many in the margins. Even if you individually identify as one of them, one of us, there is always more to be said and more solutions to be uncovered if you would only give yourself the time to ask more questions.

No, this is not the end. This book is not done. This book is a work that is rooted in the reality that we are all still a work in progress.

Gratitude Snaps

Thank you to the many reviewers of the short chapters in this book. I included your names at the top of every chapter heading because these chapters would not have been possible without your support. Your encouraging words in the margins kept me going and provided encouragement whenever I felt like giving up. This is not just my voice, but *our voice*. Additional shout-out to Jennie Magiera for helping gather this community.

Thank you, Monica Martinez, for being the first creative to call me a creative. I felt like I was officially inducted into an elite class of exceptional individuals when you first called me a creative like yourself. You're a pure creative. I'm just lucky enough to witness your brilliance on display. There was never a question about who I would ask to design my cover art. Thank you for saying yes.

Thank you, Jacquelyn Whiting. I could not imagine putting on your spectacles as you endured this entire journey with me. The reading and re-reading of my words, sometimes eye-opening, other times eye-gouging. You've read this whole text as a reviewer, editor, stylist, critic, and compassionate friend. I hope you get hired 20x over because others read these words right when they need an editor and advocate of their work. Thank you for getting me.

Thank you, Ken Shelton, for being my brother. I don't know how or why our wives put up with us, but I know that you have been the ear and the voice I have needed when no one else would quite understand. You're my big bro. Thanks for calling me at random hours throughout the day just to chat. I'm glad Brian R.

Smith was crazy enough to agree to record some of our conversations!

Thank you, most especially to my wife, Stacey. You have heard these words so many times before. You have read this book and seen its formation from the inside. You have helped wipe away my tears and listened to my pain and impassioned pontifications. Thank you for being my very best friend. I love you forever.

Thank you, Rev. Dr. Gladys Runetta Lanier, aka Mom. Two professional goals down, one more to go! Thank you for always being one step ahead of me and pushing me to keep climbing.

Thank you, God, for loving me. You have given me everything.

Endnotes

1. Laura Meckler and Kate Rabinowitz, "America's schools are more diverse than ever. But the teachers are still mostly white," The Washington Post, 27 December 2019, www.washingtonpost.com/graphics/2019/local/education/teacher-diversity/.

2. Libby Hoffman, "10 Models for design thinking," Medium, 29 July 2016, libhof.medium.com/10-models-for-design-thinking-f6943e4ee068.

3. "Educational Oppression Timeline," The Equity Collaborative, www.theequitycollaborative.com/resources/educational-oppression-timeline/. Accessed 29 January 2021.

4. "Design Thinking for Educators," IDEO, www.ideo.com/post/design-thinking-for-educators. Accessed 30 August 2021.

5. William B. Rouse, People and Organizations: Explorations of Human-Centered Design (Wiley, 2007), books.google.com/books/edition/_/42uCaj1fgpcC?hl=en&gbpv=0. Accessed 21 February 2022.

6. "Did IDEO invent design thinking?" IDEO, designthinking.ideo.com/faq/did-ideo-invent-design-thinking.

7. "PROBLEM English Definition and Meaning," Lexico, www.lexico.com/en/definition/problem. Accessed 21 January 2022.

8. Gholdy Muhammad, Cultivating Genius: An Equity Framework for Culturally and Historically Responsive Literacy (Scholastic Teaching Resources, 2020).

9. Michelle Ferrigno Warren, The Power of Proximity: Moving Beyond Awareness to Action (IVP Books, July 2017).

10. Chen Ye, "Defining Design," Medium, 3 September 2015, medium.com/hh-design/defining-the-big-d-afc856b4b8d.

11. Heather McGhee, The Sum of Us: What Racism Costs Everyone and How We Can Prosper Together (One World, 2021).

12. Tatum, Beverly. Why Are All of the Black Kids Sitting Together in the Cafeteria? Basic Books, September 2017.

13. Jeff Duncan Andrade, "Equality or Equity?" Talks at Google, 18 August 2017, www.youtube.com/watch?v=okBjLsFd58M.

14. "Definition of bias," Collins English Dictionary, www.collinsdictionary.com/us/dictionary/english/bias. Accessed 22 January 2022.

15. Tania Anaissie et al., "Liberatory Design: mindsets and modes to design for equity," static1.squarespace.com/static/60380011d63f16013f7cc4c2/t/6070b8d5c800831d97d67ff0/1618000087869/Liberatory_Design_Deck_2021.pdf.

16. Zaretta Hammond, Culturally Responsive Teaching and The Brain: Promoting Authentic Engagement and Rigor Among Culturally and Linguistically Diverse Students (Corwin, December 2014).

17. Christopher Emdin, For White Folks Who Teach in the Hood... and the Rest of Y'all Too: Reality Pedagogy and Urban Education (Beacon Press, January 2017).

18. Christopher Emdin, "Teach Teachers to Create Magic," TED, October 2013, www.ted.com/talks/christopher_emdin_teach_teachers_how_to_create_magic.

19. Keith Mays, "Dr. Monique W. Morris wants to deconstruct the stereotypes of Black girls," Ewing Marion Kauffman Foundation, 25 August 2021, www.kauffman.org/currents/deconstructing-stereotypes-of-black-girls-dr-monique-w-morris-dr-lateshia-woodley/.

20. "Project Implicit," Harvard University, implicit.harvard.edu/implicit/selectatest.html.

21. Gloria Ladson-Billings, The Dreamkeepers: Successful Teachers of African American Children, 2nd edition (Jossey-Bass, March 2009), p. 33.

22. Geneva Gay, Culturally Responsive Teaching: Theory, Research, and Practice, 3rd edition (Teachers College Press, January 2018), p. 58.

23. Barbara Miner, "Who is Backing The Bell Curve?" ASCD, 1 April 1995, www.ascd.org/el/articles/who-is-backing-the-bell-curve.

24. "Dunning-Kruger Effect," Psychology Today, www.psychologytoday.com/us/basics/dunning-kruger-effect. Accessed 24 February 2021.

25. "APA Dictionary of Psychology: bandwagon effect," American Psychological Association,

dictionary.apa.org/bandwagon-effect. Accessed 24 February 2021.

26. Iqra Noor, "Confirmation Bias," Simple Psychology, 10 June 2020, www.simplypsychology.org/confirmation-bias.html.

27. "Halo Effect," Psychology Today, www.psychologytoday.com/us/basics/halo-effect. Accessed 24 February 2021.

28. Rajiv Jhangiani and Tarry Hammond, "Ingroup Favoritism and Prejudice," Principles of Social Psychology, BCcampus, opentextbc.ca/socialpsychology/chapter/ingroup-favoritism-and-prejudice/. Accessed 24 February 2021.

29. "Choice-Supportive Bias," Academy of Advanced Thought, www.theclaritysystem.com/choice/. Accessed 24 February 2021.

30. Raymond S. Nickerson, "Confirmation Bias: A Ubiquitous Phenomenon in Many Guises," Review of General Psychology, vol. 2, no. 2, June 1998, pp. 175–220, doi:10.1037/1089-2680.2.2.175.

31. Felicia Saffold, "Bridging the Cultural Gap Between Teachers and Students," National Association of Independent Schools, Fall 2007, www.nais.org/magazine/independent-teacher/fall-2007/bridging-the-cultural-gap-between-teachers-and-stu.

32. Ladson-Billings, The Dream Keepers, p. 19.

33. "Diversity, Equity and Inclusion Glossary," University of Washington College of the Environment. environment.uw.edu/about/diversity-equity-inclusion/tools-

and-additional-resources/glossary-dei-concepts/. Accessed 13 November 2021.

34. Tatum, Beverly. Why Are All of the Black Kids Sitting Together in the Cafeteria? Basic Books, September 2017.

35. "Definition of ageism." Collins English Dictionary, collinsdictionary.com/us/dictionary/english/ageism. Accessed 13 November 2021.

36. "Definition of sexism." Collins English Dictionary, collinsdictionary.com/us/dictionary/english/sexism. Accessed 13 November 2021.

37. "Classism / Educational (in)justice." University of Cologne: Gender Equality and Diversity, 10 August 2021. vielfalt.uni-koeln.de/en/anti-discrimination/unboxingdiscrimination/classism.

38. "Definition of racism." Collins English Dictionary, collinsdictionary.com/dictionary/english/racism. Accessed 22 November 2021.

39. "Definition of ableism." Center for Disability Rights, cdrnys.org/blog/uncategorized/ableism/. Accessed 3 February 2022.

40. "Definition of colonialism." Collins English Dictionary, collinsdictionary.com/us/dictionary/english/colonialism. Accessed 22 November 2021."

41. Bendix, Aria. "The US was once a leader for healthcare and education — now it ranks 27th in the world." Business Insider, businessinsider.com/us-ranks-27th-for-healthcare-and-education-2018-9. 27 September 2018.

42. "It's just everywhere - sexism in schools," National Education Union, 17 January 2019, neu.org.uk/advice/its-just-everywhere-sexism-schools.

43. Toldson, Ivory A., Tyne McGee, and Brianna P. Lemmons. "Reducing Suspensions by Improving Academic Engagement among School-age Black Males." Howard University. civilrightsproject.ucla.edu/resources/projects/center-for-civil-rights-remedies/school-to-prison-folder/state-reports/copy3_of_dignity-disparity-and-desistance-effective-restorative-justice-strategies-to-plug-the-201cschool-to-prison-pipeline/toldson-reducing-suspension-ccrr-conf-2013.pdf

44. Coates, Ta-Nehisi. Between the World and Me. Spiegel & Grau, 2015.

45. Wilkerson, Isabel. Caste: The Origins of Our Discontents. Random House, 2020.

46. Magee, Rhonda V. The Inner Work of Racial Justice. Penguin Publishing Group, 2019.

47. Ibrim X. Kendi, How to Be an Antiracist. One World, 2019.

48. Oluo, Ijeoma. So You Want to Talk About Race. Seal Press, 2018.

49. Hirshfield, Laura E. "Tokenism." Wiley Online Library. 30 December 2015, onlinelibrary.wiley.com/doi/abs/10.1002/9781118663202.wberen199.

50. Glaser, Jack. "What Is Racial Profiling?" Suspect Race: Causes and Consequences of Racial Profiling, Oxford Scholarship Online. 2014.

oxford.universitypressscholarship.com/view/10.1093/acprof:
oso/9780195370409.001.0001/acprof-9780195370409-
chapter-1.

51. "Diversity, Equity and Inclusion Glossary," University of
Washington College of the Environment.
environment.uw.edu/about/diversity-equity-inclusion/tools-
and-additional-resources/glossary-dei-concepts/. Accessed
13 November 2021.

52. Saad, Layla. Me and White Supremacy: Combat Racism,
Change the World, and Become a Good Ancestor.
Sourcebooks, 2020.

53. Steele, Claude M. "Thin Ice: Stereotype Threat and Black
College Students," The Atlantic. August 1999.

54. "Diversity, Equity and Inclusion Glossary," University of
Washington College of the Environment. Accessed 13
November 2021.

55. "Martin Luther King, Jr. at Oberlin," Oberlin College Archives.
www2.oberlin.edu/external/EOG/BlackHistoryMonth/MLK/K
ingAutograph.html.

56. Sue, Derald Wing, ed. Microaggressions and Marginality:
Manifestation, Dynamics, and Impact. United Kingdom:
Wiley, 2010.

57. Brownicity. "Tribe Vibe: Makers Of Safe Spaces."
brownicity.com/blog/trive-vibe-makers-of-safe-spaces/.
Accessed 1 December 2021.

58. "What Is Voter Suppression?" FindLaw, 7 August 2020,
findlaw.com/voting/how-do-i-protect-my-right-to-vote-
/what-is-voter-suppression-.html.

59. "What Is Censorship?" American Civil Liberties Union. aclu.org/other/what-censorship. Accessed 13 November 2021.

60. "Housing Inequality." Urban Sociology. rampages.us/urban/housing-inequality/. Accessed 13 November 2021.

61. "Criminal Justice." Cornell University Legal Information Institute. law.cornell.edu/wex/criminal_justice. Accessed 15 November 2021.

62. "Police Brutality Law and Legal Definition." USLegal, Inc. definitions.uslegal.com/p/police-brutality/. Accessed 15 November 2021.

63. Martin, Jermeelah. "Solutions for Education Inequality." United for a Fair Economy. 25 August 2020, www.faireconomy.org/solutions_for_education_inequality.

64. Love, Bettina L. We Want to Do More Than Survive: Abolitionist Teaching and the Pursuit of Educational Freedom. Beacon Press, 2019.

65. Freire, Paulo. Education for Critical Consciousness. Continuum International Publishing Group, 2005.

66. Freire, Paulo. Pedagogy of the Oppressed. Continuum, 1970.

67. "The History of Police Brutality." The National Trial Lawyers Top 100. 27 July 2020. thenationaltriallawyers.org/2020/07/the-history-of-american-police-brutality/.

68. "Police Brutality: A Prisoner was shamefully beaten by
    Officers, he was Kicked and Pounded in a Cell ---Probably
    Fatally Injured." Chicago Daily Tribune. 12 October 1872.

Made in United States
North Haven, CT
17 April 2023

35566543R00091